THE BACK DOOR

AN ENTREPRENEUR'S GUIDE TO FINDING A
WAY TO SUCCESS THAT YOU DIDN'T KNOW
EXISTED

ISHAN GOEL

ISBN: 978-1-951407-76-6 paperback

ISBN: 978-1-951407-72-8 ebook   ·

WAKE UP

You can change the lives of millions. Depending on how soon you found this book, it might even be billions.

I promise you there is absolutely no difference between you, me and any successful person other than experience and mindset. I was never the smartest person in the room, but some of the smartest people I know worked for the people I learned from. Over time, I realized the system I was in was positioning me to be part of the 99 percent rather than the one percent.

No grade, award or recognition in the early years of your life—especially within the schooling system—remotely even matters. This isn't a book on school reform, but it is for anyone who has the drive and determination to get out of the systems that are failing them. This book is for the lost ones who feel like they can't do anything or who need guidance to unlock their true potential. For others, this book will be a road map to unlocking doors you didn't even know existed.

Welcome to the Back Door.

DISCLAIMER

All our lives are guided by choices—just like the choice you made to pick up this book. So many people look for handouts in life, but the truth is your path is determined by *you* and you alone. The second you start taking too much input from your parents, teachers, friends or whoever else, you start down a path that isn't authentically owned by you. So as you read, ask yourself: *Why am I reading this?* Without the right why, you may be wasting your time.

Before you get in too deep, know this book doesn't have any get-rich-quick schemes. It will not lead you to a pot of gold. It is simply a map—my map. You can learn and take notes from it, but you can't copy it entirely.

Lastly, I ask one thing: don't make this book just another impulse purchase collecting dust on your shelf. Embark on reading this when you're ready to commit. Only start reading if you're ready to finish what you start.

INTRODUCTION

The back door doesn't exist. You need to create it in your head.

So what is the back door? It's the secret way into the buildings and rooms you want to be in that only you can access, figuratively speaking. It's a way of not listening to other people's standards and tapping into your own genius to create pathways for you to advance. It's the realization that you can use your unique strengths to impact the world and make your visions come to life—regardless of the obstacles and limitations in your path.

When you find your own back doors to success, you'll realize that your limitations are like the chair in the picture. You feel bound by them, but they have no power over your reality. Without a doubt, there are limitations on you right now (also known as limiting beliefs). They are things you've told yourself, been told or been forced to accept because of people around you.

What if I told you that you are in full control of all of those beliefs and can change them to help you instead of hurt you? Doing so will unlock your back door. Most people who find success are not geniuses—they're just crazy enough to chase after their goals and believe in themselves. They are the ones willing to fail faster and harder than anyone else.

Everyone has their own success limitations, and they can be well hidden. As we go through life, those limitations change and evolve. The important thing is to focus on finding them and breaking through them. Doing so will give you full control over your own reality, no matter how crazy or outlandish your goals are—you just have to put the time, energy and focus into achieving your goals.

This book will give you the tools to do that, but first you have to believe that you can achieve whatever you want. In short, this book will amplify your ability to get ahead of the curve.

In life, people tend to take the easy way out or accept systems that are already in place. Instead, we need to find our own keys to success and our own back doors to make our lives more efficient. Instead of blindly following other people's footsteps, we can make our own path—and we can shed all of the labels people try to put on us along the way.

I've been lucky enough to meet many extremely talented people and learn the way they think and operate. In this book, I hope to give anyone who feels stuck in a system the tools to take control of their own lives, follow their passions and become successful. To that end, I want to share an internal success formula that one of my mentors shared with me.

To be truly internally successful, you need to do five things:

1. Decide what you want out of life. There are plenty of entrepreneurs out there who have an internal itch for more, but they're not sure how to scratch it or what giving in to that urge would entail. Before you can live your dreams, you need to know what they are—and make the choices necessary to achieve them.

2. Commit to your decision to get what you want out of life. I'm talking about total commitment. It's easy to become temporarily inspired or lifted by your emotions in the short term, but what keeps most people from real, lasting success is that they don't put in the hard work when that high wears off. To succeed, you have to stay on your path and see it through, all the way to the end.

3. Be willing to sacrifice things for your higher vision. This can mean sacrificing your time with friends, with family or your hobbies, or it can mean sacrificing money and energy for a bigger purpose. The most successful people know that achieving higher and higher levels of success requires equal amounts of sacrifice.

4. Work your ass off. Plenty of people have talent and good ideas, but they don't have the discipline to see them through. You don't want to be one of those people. The people who are really successful aren't born geniuses or the most talented.

They're the people who are most dedicated and who work the smartest.

5. Be persistent and persevere. In Napoleon Hill's classic book *Think and Grow Rich*, he talks about a Colorado miner who moved across the country to get rich mining gold. After mining for months and months and coming up empty-handed, he quits —but what he doesn't know is he only had three more feet to dig before he would've struck gold. This is the most important lesson: don't give up and allow the fear of failure to win. Keep trying and keep going, at all costs.

Even if this is all straightforward, we need to remind ourselves to follow these principles day in and day out. If we do, we can be sure that we'll stay in the game for the long haul. After all, no career flourishes overnight—and mine is no exception. It started by identifying what I wanted, finding mentors, moving into my passions and expanding my network from there. My system of success had to be built from the ground up.

The back doors in life are always hidden, but by pursuing your passion and finding your true purpose, they will appear in whatever you're doing. It is your choice to open those doors and make the most of them, even though many of us ignore them. After all, why wait at the front door as opportunities pass you by when you could get in easier through the back?

With that said, I'm going to offer you everything I know on how to do the same thing in your life, in your way. I'm going to take you through all my fundamental beliefs and perspectives before showing how I apply them all to my life. From there, I'll get more specific about how to grow your own business and live a meaningful life. With everything in place, my hope is that you will start to find your own back doors to success—and the life of your dreams.

Do not let schooling get in the way of your education.

CONTENTS

PART I

LIFE

"Lead me, follow me, or get out of my way."

-George Patton

CHAPTER 1

UNDERSTAND YOURSELF

When you truly understand yourself and who you are at a deep level, you will become more in tune with everything else.

Know Thyself, and You Shall Win

To this day, I clearly remember sitting in French class in one of those chairs connected to the desk and staring up at the whiteboard while the teacher slowly explained the same thing the same way, just like the day before. I was only 14, but I was stuck in a loop that would start back over again from scratch every day. I remember thinking: *This can't be it. This can't be all there is to life. There has to be more.* It felt like I was running out the clock on life—all while carrying the aching weight of not knowing what the future held for me.

I was jealous of how easily others finished their assignments, and it started to make me feel small. Having issues reading because of a mild case of dyslexia made reading both boring and frustrating, and I was getting sick and tired of all the repetition. None of my classes were making an impression on me, except some parts of history and science. At the same time, I wanted to succeed because I wanted to have an impact on the world. I didn't want to give up. It was as my parents always told me: education is everything.

School felt like a trap to me, but it was also my entire life at that moment. More and more, I realized the educational system was a weight I just couldn't carry—it was about to break me. Even though I always thought of myself as someone who didn't give up on anything, after a while, it started to feel like a game I didn't want to keep playing. I wanted to play an entirely new game that I would design myself. Meanwhile, outside of school, I had already begun investing my time in the world of business and entrepreneurship.

It all started in fifth grade. This is the day my life changed course forever. Schools always bring in those fancy school keynote speakers, but this time it was different. Diana S. Zimmerman came to talk about her series *Kandide*. She was touring the country to promote her message, talking to kids about life's challenges and how to deal with bullies. Diana was a published author, the owner of a large marketing agency and an entrepreneur who learned magic as a kid to turn herself into one of the world's best "lady magicians." In school that day, she told us the key to success in life was to find an outlet to connect not just to the things you loved but also with yourself.

A lot of people in the assembly weren't paying attention that day, but I was mesmerized. She seemed like a superhero to my fifth-grade self. All the people I knew lived regular lives doing normal jobs—meanwhile, this woman used her passion to make another life for herself, and I needed to understand how. I'd been writing books on my own time before that assembly and had dreams of becoming the next J.K. Rowling. Now, Diana was showing me that it didn't have to stay a fantasy.

Right after the assembly was over, I made my first email account to get in touch with her directly, and she became my first mentor.

From: ISHAN GOEL
Sent: Fri 5/7/2010 8:58 PM
To: Diana S. Zimmerman
Subject: coppell texas denton creek Ishan goel [time portal]

Hi my name is ishan and i talked to you for 5 min at denton creek elementry. You said i could email you my story. love to write and make up magical things i did not get the time to talk at school my teachers were call my class i would love if you could read the Time Portal and email me back or call me at 972 ▓ ▓ or 972 ▓ ▓ i would love to here back !

Ishan Goel
Coppell Texas

> *This is an email I wrote at 11 years old to my first mentor, Diana S.*
> *Zimmerman.*

I told her I was writing a book called *Time Portal*, a magical tale about two siblings who found a portal to other worlds in their library that froze time in the real world.

I'd been working on the first 25 to 30 pages of it for a year and sent it all to her.

All Water - Part 1
By: ISHAN GOEL

© 2010. IG Publications Inc. ™

Sure enough, she took the time to go through it and interact with it—and it made me feel like the biggest person in the world. After that, Diana and I were in touch constantly. I wrote her hundreds and hundreds of emails, and she always wrote back. I sought her advice on my own goals and career choices. She became a role model to me because she lived in her own mystical world that she'd created by herself, and I wanted to do the same.

Over the past 11 years, Diana and I have exchanged thousands of emails.
Here is a screenshot of only some of the emails.

What Diana showed me was how powerful communication and stories can be in determining our lives.

In school, I saw how the system's bad communication could keep talented kids bored, trapped and boxed in. Outside of it, I saw how good communicators were getting rich and changing the world according to their own vision. Seeing the bigger picture, I decided to look at the situation differently. If I was going to be successful, I would have to do it my way through good communication—with myself, with the rest of the world and in translating my dreams into reality. Still, the first step in that process would be to shake off all the negative labels that had been put on me and start writing my own.

From that day forward, I saw I was being told two competing stories. In the first one, I was in school following all the rules, feeling trapped and bored learning things I didn't care about. In the other, I was making my way in the world as an entrepreneur, learning things I was truly interested in, finding clients and building something for myself.

I was starting to understand the bigger picture. The school system was handing out T-shirts that were the same size for everyone and expecting them all to fit—and if they didn't fit, they would stretch or shrink them until they did. Some kids fit in the shirts perfectly, and others were shrinking themselves trying to fit—or else they were giving up completely. I was being told time and time again I was going to fail, and I was close to giving up.

Key & Important Takeaways:

- You are not what people and systems say about you.
- You are a product of your own mindset and what you believe in.
- There is not one way to succeed; you are free to find what works for you.

Use Labels to Your Advantage

As I learned early on, people put labels on everything in life. They put them on things they love and things they hate, things they want to continue and things they want to stop. At a deep level, we use labels to think and communicate—and the way we label things in our heads ends up affecting how we see them in real life.

Even if labels affect our lives, the actual labels themselves aren't real—they're just sets of suggestions, opinions and programs we keep running. They're not real in the same way the boundaries set by parents and society aren't real. Ultimately, they are guidelines that are there to keep people without a clear path or purpose in life.

Labeling applies to everything in life, but it applies to school especially: there's a baseline curriculum, and it's supposed to work for everyone. Still, because the school system is built for the masses, it comes with goals that are designed for anybody to achieve. For people with bigger visions and dreams for their lives, that can be a problem—but it's also often a problem for the people who *do* get good grades.

Some kids might be able to follow instructions, do the work and get B+'s, but they'll still come out unprepared for the real world. School isn't designed to be an environment where kids can thrive as individuals and be creative. It's a place that zeroes out the possibility for real creativity, growth and flexibility, because without a rigid system in place, there would be no way for teachers and administrators to measure and standardize performance.

To me, being in school was like being a car on a superhighway stuck in gridlock traffic, unable to explore or move out of my lane. It was a place that handed labels to students and told them to stick with them for life instead of encouraging them to change the labels or throw them out entirely.

Think of the first time you gave a big presentation in class—and you blew it. It was a peak negative emotional experience, and you told yourself right there that public speaking was bad. The experience was one of pain and embarrassment, emotions we all want to avoid. To deal with that, you mentally wrote a label for it: *public speaking = bad/scary.*

It's a funny thing that public speaking is one of so many people's top fears because I created a different label for it. Public speaking is adrenaline. It's my version of sky-diving. I get a high off of being in front of a crowd of people because I have the room in the palm of my hand. Still, all of that description is just another kind of label—a positive one. Even if it could've had a negative label, I turned it into something positive instead to help me perform better—and you can too.

We all have hundreds and thousands of labels for everything in life, and the voice we hear in our heads about those labels makes up our self-communication. That voice can be positive or negative depending on what we choose to make them, but if we identify the labels that are hurting us, we can choose to change them and shift our entire perspective for the better.

At my eighth-grade science fair, I used this trick to my advantage. Even though it was a local competition that was just at my school, I was so confident I would win that I printed out the state qualifying paperwork ahead of time. By doing so, I told myself: *you've got this.*

When the day of the competition came, everyone else was caught up in the stress of the moment—but I was already picturing being on a national stage. The result was I ended up moving on to States on the strength of my science project, and it was more proof of what I knew: self-communication and positive labels on the inside become real on the outside.

There's a famous quote that I live by: "It's not what you say, it's how you say it." I use it a lot in marketing today, but it applies to everything. Effective communication starts from within and flows out of you. It means you have to get clear on who you are and stand firm in it rather than letting the world determine who you are.

In life, it's all about tapping into your ability to do things you love—and learning you can do things how you want, when you want and how you want. The way society communicates is to put boundaries on everything, but all those boundaries are completely breakable.

Key & Important Takeaways:

- We put labels on everything in life, but the labels aren't set in stone and can be reset.
- When we're aware of our labels, we can choose to change them.
- With the right labels, we can turn our fears into positives.

Failure Is Helpful

The best thing I learned in school was how to fail because it helped me realize all the labels I thought were real were actually bullshit. Failing and not being ruined by it meant the whole system was a lie. It meant I could reshape my destiny, and it went way beyond school. It was about me as a person. Unfortunately, a lot of people are stuck in the school system getting by without experiencing real failure, which can come back to hurt you in hard times.

I knew a kid in high school who was a high-performing student. He got straight A's in everything he did academically and was great at whatever he tried. High school was his playground, and he was on top of the world. The word "failure" wasn't in his dictionary.

Reality started to settle in as he graduated and went to college. He had to apply to colleges and compete in a much bigger pool, and he had to apply for jobs that were in high demand. He started experiencing his first taste of failure later, and it was a shock to his system—he started feeling like he was becoming a part of the crowd like everyone else, and he wanted to go back to being a star in a less competitive arena. The school system had set up kids like him not to fail, and because of that, he had never learned how to fail correctly.

When my friend failed at one of his college business ventures, he got extremely depressed and started using substances to numb the pain. He hadn't learned to fail early, and he internalized labels that became roadblocks to his future success. Time and time again, he would deny reality and describe his failed businesses as "successful." It wasn't only that he couldn't embrace failure; he couldn't confront it, either.

So many people in life like to have things to fall back on. It's why a lot of parents try to get their kids to go to college (basically a backup plan: anyone who goes to college will have a degree to fall back on). Parents want kids to prepare for the future and to learn things that will help them get into better colleges and careers. What they're really doing is building in safety nets and cementing a lack of self-confidence and self-sufficiency.

It's a plan that says you're going to fail and that you should be prepared when you do, but the logic of it sets you up to fail backward. But I don't want to fail *backward*—what's the point of that? I want to fail *forward* trying new things and not following a plan that already exists. That way, I make at least some progress and can plan my next jump accordingly. Embracing safety nets is another way of saying you don't have faith in what you're doing. And that doubt will kill your goals faster than anything else.

Key & Important Takeaways:

- Never failing can be more damaging than just failing.
- You should not be afraid of failure; you should embrace it.
- Relying on safety nets and backup plans leads to failing backward and losing progress.
- Pursuing a passion and a dream helps you fail forward—and into better things.

CHAPTER 2

KNOW YOUR VALUE

One of my first memories is going on a field trip and coming face to face with a painting of a huge glacier. It was so vivid and real—and because I was so small, the painting towered above me. I could feel all the sensations coming off the painting like it was really in the room. The air around me felt crisp, and I could swear I was getting a chill. From that moment on, I was hooked on art.

Right away, I wanted to start painting. I remember spending long days gripping a brush in my hand until it was sore, thinking about all the possibilities of a blank piece of paper and then splashing bright streaks of color down. I kept painting and got better and better and even entered a city-wide contest in second grade. The painting I did made it into the newspaper, and I swelled with pride.

In my first experiences with painting, I didn't overthink things; even when I entered the competition, my only intention was to do my best and share my creativity. I wanted to be part of the world of art. As I got older, that interest in painting started to fade and transformed into a passion for photography when I was about 14 or 15. Even so, painting definitely shaped how I approached taking pictures.

Good photography can be just as powerful as painting. In a way, they're not that different. When I was learning to paint, the main thing I had to learn was that a good painting was all about what you added in—what elements you put onto the canvas. With photography, it was almost the opposite. The most powerful photographs were so powerful because of what the photographer chose to leave out.

Before long, I was taking pictures everywhere I went, and I started to figure I could use my photography skills to make some money. I tried to find clients, but even though I knew the basics of the craft, I didn't know much about running a business. I figured I should start off simple by learning from someone who was already doing what I wanted to do.

I went on Google and typed in "photographers near me." Five or six people came up, and I reached out to all of them. One by one, I left voicemails, saying something along the lines of:

"I've seen your work, and I'd like to work with you. I've been taking photos for a while, I love photography, and I can't wait to add value to whatever you're doing at your events."

Above all else, my priority was to try to add value immediately.

A few weeks went by, and someone reached out to me asking if I could help edit their photos. I didn't know anything about photo editing, so I ended up failing on that one. Fortunately, someone else reached out afterward with an opportunity I was qualified for. His name was Nick Mallouf, a photographer based out of Dallas, Texas, and he offered to sit down with me at a coffee shop to talk and go over some photographs.

After our first meeting at the coffee shop, we started working together right away. What I didn't know was that Nick would become a mentor to me. He brought me to events with him and let me shoot with him and afterward, we would sit together and go through the photos we took. He picked out which ones were good, which ones were bad and what I could learn from each one. I was getting more and more experience, and my confidence was growing. Before long, I was doing it on my own.

I launched a nice website for myself and made some professional branding to go along with it. I got myself a decent camera with a bunch of money I'd saved, and I jumped into that world completely. Though I had bigger dreams to run a business that would include marketing and branding and everything else, I decided to stay focused just on photos. After all, I figured it would be easier for clients to trust a 14-year-old photographer than it would be to trust a 14-year-old marketing expert—at least for a little while.

Key & Important Takeaways:

- Following your passions can show you connections others don't see.
- When you have an interest or passion, act on it right away.
- Introduce yourself to mentors and experts—and offer them value right away.

Your Self-Worth Is Your Power

Right away, I saw there was a big difference between photography for personal and business events. At personal events, I would get dragged all over the place. People would pull on my T-shirt, bump into me, ruin my shots and yell at me to do whatever they wanted. Clients treated me like an employee, a worker or a servant. At business events, it was totally different. I was just like everyone else. I was dressed like everyone else, and I was "in the room" just like everyone else was. Once I saw that, I knew where I had to focus my energy.

I realized that I had to value my own time and my own self-worth enough to focus only on event photography. While I was helping my mentor on his own shoots, I also set up my own company: Ishan Goel Photography.

My experience with Nick kept me away from weddings and other personal shoots that were more of a pain than they were worth. It meant I had to take on cheaper clients and give up a lot of money in the short term, but I knew I didn't want to do weddings or birthday parties—they wouldn't help me move forward in my career. I realized that if I did what I loved and I stayed in that lane, the money would come naturally. As a result, I made my first $50,000 from photography between the ages of 14 and 16, all by keeping things as simple as possible.

My business was growing through word-of-mouth, and before long, I was doing fewer and fewer shoots with Nick and doing more of my own. One of my first exclusive deals was shooting photography for my high school's sports teams, but soon after I started shooting business events where I met pro athletes, CEOs of companies, artists and other inspiring people.

When I was 16, I got a contract to do photography for the Dallas Marathon—and they were surprised to see how young I was when I showed up! The beautiful thing was for that event, I hired my mentor back and built a team of my friends around me to help out like Nick had done for me. The whole time, the goal was simple: make every photo tell a story.

That event was a huge boost of self-confidence, and it showed my growth in team building, providing value and communicating. Along the way, I had to learn so many business skills like how to invoice, how to manage teams, how to find price points that made sense and how to upsell clients. Of course, the other part was learning from missed opportunities because I was scared to ask for more money or to offer more services.

Photography was all teaching me what I needed to know to be an entrepreneur—I could do what I wanted to do. I could run a business and ask for whatever I needed, and the worst that could happen was someone would say no. That mindset put me in the frame of mind to allow the right people to say yes as naturally as possible. All of it was building up a sense of self-worth—and it was opening doors to even bigger opportunities.

Key & Important Takeaways:

- Knowing your worth helps you make better strategic decisions.
- Develop self-worth by focusing on activities you get the most out of.
- By doing this, your skills and reputation will develop, and you'll get bigger opportunities.

Gain Confidence by Letting Go

If you're not confident, people can detect it. They can see it in the way you stand and the way you say things. In business and networking, the old me would always ask a ton of questions and talk over people until I felt like I was sure I'd said everything I needed to say. I was following a faulty label that said "control equals confidence." Over time, I realized it was more powerful to let go of some of the control. Allowing other people's input would help determine what actions I could take.

When going into situations that are uncharted territory, most people try to control them or label them in a way that makes them feel familiar (even if the label is inaccurate). By doing that, they're only tying their feet together instead of letting themselves learn in the moment. As I learned, being comfortable with uncertainty is a big part of life and of entrepreneurship.

To achieve big things, you have to sacrifice a lot early on—including friendships, birthday parties and distractions. You pour all your energy into looking towards the future, and you often have to risk looking like you don't know what you're talking about. It makes it harder to find like-minded people, and it can be lonely and confusing, but it's all part of the process.

As I've learned firsthand, a lot of people struggle with what to do first when it comes to big ideas. For me, the hesitation comes down to a lack of self-confidence or self-worth. Plenty of people tell themselves things like "I can't do that" or "I'm too young" when they're getting ready to follow their dreams, but by doing that, they end up losing opportunities immediately and setting themselves up for failure. Their internal operating systems are running negative programs, and those programs become self-fulfilling prophecies.

When people think like that, confidence doesn't flow because there's something inside holding it back from expressing itself. Appreciating your own value takes time, but it doesn't come from thinking your problems to death—it comes from taking action over and over again. Identifying those internal blockages is so important to boosting your confidence, but it's not enough just to identify them. You have to take action to remove them and to live out the life of your dreams.

Key & Important Takeaways:

- Being "in control" is not the same as being confident.
- True confidence comes from being comfortable with uncertainty.
- Deep confidence doesn't come overnight; it comes through repeated practice.

CHAPTER 3

MASTER YOUR HAPPINESS

With my photography business succeeding, I decided to keep seeking out entrepreneurs and mentors who could help me grow. Though I was making more connections and getting some great opportunities, I started getting the same advice from people: "Be humble."

I started to realize that I was working for a lot of entrepreneurs who were playing that game with me. Every time I'd achieve something, I would get the same pat on the back. "Good job," they would say, "keep going." On one level, I knew I was doing really good work for them—but it seemed like no matter what I did, I never fully arrived.

It was advice meant to keep me from getting too big for my boots, but it meant that I was always looking for the next thing. I was always stretching for the next accomplishment, trying to impress my mentors and get their admiration. Even though I kept pushing, I started to realize the feeling I was looking for was never going to come.

The entire experience started to give me a sense of imposter syndrome. Even when I achieved something huge, I wouldn't embrace it—instead, I would say I just got lucky or deny my accomplishments some other way. I would do whatever it took to say what I'd done wasn't good enough or that it could be better somehow. I was stripping myself of all my achievements. As I came to realize, "be humble" was okay advice for people who needed encouragement to keep looking forward—but it was also a great technique to keep ambitious people trapped working for you.

I had to take a moment to look at what I was actually accomplishing. A project I'd just finished had made $100,000 in 24 hours for one of my clients and his business. On top of that, his company was getting interviews and articles published in top magazines, all of which I'd helped facilitate. Even though I was doing all that, my work wasn't being acknowledged in any way. I felt a lack of control, and I was getting frustrated, which was understandable—but I was still doing amazing things.

The problem was a loss of perspective. It wasn't an issue with me; it was an issue on the other side that the people I was working for didn't know how to show praise and appreciation. What I should've been doing was celebrating my small wins and staying focused on the progress I was making. Instead, I wasn't giving myself any credit and was only raising the bar higher for myself, which was making me burn out.

I knew that to keep going forward, I couldn't internalize that. Instead, I could focus on my wins—and I could celebrate them on my own.

Key & Important Takeaways:

- "Being humble" can be good, but not at the expense of your self-esteem.
- Despite your ambitions, always remember what you've already accomplished.
- Whenever you get a win, acknowledge it and celebrate it.

Celebrate the Smallest Wins

Before I started a photography business, I knew I wanted more money to spend. I wanted an income for myself so I didn't have to ask my parents for everything, so my first plan was to apply at local restaurants, which were Taco Bell and Panda Express. Walking into each one, I saw the starting pay was only $8 an hour—but the managers' pay was $15. Even though I didn't have any experience, I applied for manager jobs at both places. I didn't get either job, but I was still satisfied that I had the ambition to try to do big things.

After connecting with Nick and getting started in photography, my starting level wage was $25 an hour—and at 14 or 15 years old, that was a huge number. I was shocked by it—most people my age were making $6 or $7 an hour, and here I was jumping to $25 right away without much experience.

My mentor was making a lot more than that, sure, but I was learning—I was helping his business, and he was coaching me on how to have a better eye and how to run my own events. To him, it was just an opportunity to streamline things, but to me, it was my entire business! Regardless, I still had to celebrate what seemed like an outrageous amount of money. It set my bar high, and I knew a normal job would never be enough from that point on.

Getting last-minute text messages from Nick that we had new jobs was the best feeling in the world. Any time he would send me the specs for a new job, I would start doing the math. I might work from 8 am to 2:30 pm, which would come out to $212.50 at the rate I was getting. I divided that by the Texas minimum wage, and it came out to 28 hours of work—but I was only working six and a half! I was still trading my time for money, but it was at such a high level. I was taking photos and beating the salaries of people fresh out of college, making more than entry-level pharmacists!

As I worked with Nick, I was busy every weekend and was always pushing myself. My wage moved from $25 to $30, then $30 to $35 and eventually all the way up to $50 an hour—and I celebrated every increment along the way. Eventually, Nick let me go to events by myself when I got my driver's license, and I panicked on the highways driving across town in new locations in high-speed traffic with so much expensive equipment in the car (plus I had to be on time—no matter what). After a while, I was showing up to events and running them all on my own— and hiring my friends to help me out. I got some of my photos in a local coffee shop to advertise myself and dropped off a bunch of business cards—and when the bowl was empty, I celebrated again.

My visibility and track record were increasing my business, and it gave me the confidence I needed to keep going. I realized I was winning when I got one of my first huge event paychecks and realized I would have to pay $4,000 of it back to my team! I remember holding onto the check for just a few days longer, imagining it was all profit that I'd get to keep (which is a bit counter-productive in retrospect—teamwork is what makes so much of success possible). I just wanted to hold the check a little longer and visualize the next milestone, so giving it away was a little painful. Still, nobody keeps 100 percent of anything.

The point is you never want to lose sight of your accomplishments, or you'll burn out—and there are always things to celebrate. To get in that mindset, you have to learn to set small milestones towards your goals that you can celebrate—otherwise, you can fall victim to "big map syndrome."

If you look at a map of the whole planet, where you are is always going to look small by comparison. The same goes for your achievements. If you're only looking forward to the day when you'll own a mansion, you'll miss all the progress you make on the way. When you achieve things, you have to give yourself credit for actually achieving them! That way, as you get a string of small wins going, they start adding up to bigger wins.

Key & Important Takeaways:

- Always stretch yourself towards the biggest opportunities.
- To keep a positive attitude, celebrate every positive milestone no matter how small.
- Avoid the "big map syndrome" of setting unrealistic expectations by only comparing yourself to who you were yesterday.

Give Yourself Permission

You can't wait for something to change to get permission to do the things you want to do. You have to just do them. Negativity holds people back from doing what they want, whether it's because they're scared or because they don't know what to do or how to do it. In my experience, I was all about jumping in, learning what I could and experimenting. I didn't wait for any signs, and I didn't wait for anything to happen. I just jumped in.

By putting my ego to the side, I was able to test out different things to see what worked and what didn't. Though I try to forget about them now, I worked my way through so many bad birthday parties with kids screaming and parents berating me for not being fast enough. No matter how painful and irritating those times were, they taught me important lessons about ego.

I'm not saying you can just show up as a beginner and act like you know more than the experts in your field—I'm saying the opposite. When I got into photography, I didn't think of myself as a professional photographer. I had to be willing to open up and ask for help to take my business to the next level. I went to events and did my best to blend in. Instead of telling myself I didn't belong there, I acted like I did. It was a lesson I picked up from Nick. In his studio, he has a poster hanging up with a sentence I still think about:

"It's better done than perfect."

By taking some action, you can build your ego and your self-worth in a healthy way to protect yourself and your interests. In my case, by having those negative experiences I realized I didn't need to let people step on me to follow my dreams and grow my career. I had to acknowledge that my value was important—and that I was allowed to put my foot down. After working with so many people, I realized there were good clients out there as well. There were people who hired me because they trusted my vision and respected me and who wanted the best for everyone involved. They had a win-win attitude. Those were the people I wanted to be in business with.

Even if we have a fear of failure or of taking risks and looking like an idiot, getting started is the most important thing you can do. School teaches us to learn some unchanging curriculum, and college mostly does more of the same. Even if it's more interesting than high school, college is still a safety net —you're learning to be a cog in someone else's machine.

Because we have so much training in following what other people want to do versus what we want to do, it can take practice to break out of those habits. With practice, you can get more grounded in yourself and increase your confidence and self-esteem to do what you want to do.

At the end of the day, it's all about balance. It's good to swallow your ego at times, but it's also good to put your foot down to stabilize yourself in the right circumstances. Never forget that you have worth, your time has worth and your work has worth. You can't let people mistreat you or not pay you. In some circumstances, doing a little free work or making a financial sacrifice might be worth considering if you know it'll benefit you in the long run—but make sure you think long and hard about it.

Key & Important Takeaways:

- Jumping in and experimenting is always better than waiting around.
- No matter the specific outcomes, taking action will always get you experience.
- The permission you're waiting for will never come— so give it to yourself.

Don't Be the Unhappy Millionaire

I was once at a self-help business seminar with about 350 people attending, many of whom were invited to stand up and share their experiences. One of the people who stood up was a multi-millionaire. He grabbed the mic and started talking:

"I did everything I wanted to do in life. I have a car, a house, a great family and a thriving business. But I'm still not happy."

Despite his success, he got onstage and broke down crying. Everyone in the crowd could hear in his voice how sad he was. As he kept talking, it was clear the only time he was happy when he was working. He got so immersed in the process of launching a new product or new service that once it ended, he would get depressed again. He was so fixated on achieving things that he never lived in the moment or appreciated what he already had. It was proof to me: financial success doesn't automatically make you happy.

It was good he had the courage to admit how he felt, but he'd made a mistake in his thinking. He was coming at it all wrong, and I knew because I could relate.

The truth is entrepreneurs go through an evolution of success. At first, you start off oriented to the goal at the end of the process—you want the mansion or the car or the status, and you'll work as hard as you can to get it. In the next stage, you get process-oriented—it's not about the car or the mansion anymore, it's about loving being in the flow of working and creating, being immersed in your passion where the money is just a nice byproduct. Though it may be better than only being goal-oriented (and most people don't even get there), it's still possible to get lost in the process as well.

For this millionaire, every accomplishment he had was the end of his hard work, the end of his process—and he was confusing that ending as a negative. I thought of it in terms of working hard on a video for YouTube, for example. You spend plenty of time planning it, 12 hours shooting it, more hours editing it, fixing the audio and so on. The process is thrilling, and you're loving the work—but when you post it, it's all over. You're back to square one, and everything goes dark. You could even say the same thing for watching a great TV show and getting to the last episode.

Everyone goes through that period of detachment from something they've invested so much time in, and it's easy to confuse that feeling of sadness as "I hate my work" or "I hate my life." But that's not true—you love the process, and you love building things; you're just going through an emotional cycle. You have to recognize that your love of building things and being in the flow is your superpower and encourage yourself to pick up another project—but to keep balance by knowing everything has to come to an end, but you can always start again.

The other half of this lesson came after I'd had success and started traveling all over the world. Right away, I was going everywhere I ever wanted to go—India, China and countless other places. After seeing all these different countries, I noticed how different their cultures and values were. They all had very different approaches to happiness. What was clear, though, was that happiness was not only related to material gain and that it could be found anywhere.

I met happy people who were living in slums, and at the same time, I knew millionaires back home struggling with addiction. I started to see happiness wasn't really one choice, it was a state of mind created by many personal choices. I noticed that the more we chose things that we didn't want to do but "needed" to do, the more it led to unhappiness. It was a pattern that affected all other parts of life as well.

Long-term unhappiness can come from a lack of drive, addiction, career blockages and an inability to grow. It can come from being cut off from relationships or not being in control of our time. When you look at it that way, happiness is simple—but it's not easy. Even if all you have to do is do the opposite of all the above, it's still tough to maintain every day.

Of everyone in my life, my mentor, Joe Polish of Genius Network, has given me the best lessons about happiness:

"There's no such thing as simply being happy or successful. It is a matter of having certain things in your life. You're being successful when you have certain things related to health, to relationships, to money, to career, to whatever allows you to be engaged. Happiness is really being in a flow state, being connected and putting yourself in a position where you can respond to life rather than react to life."

Seeing the way Joe lives his life, it's hard to disagree with him. This way is better because it doesn't make happiness one big thing you have to master at once. It's a lot of different important parts, and we make a lot of hard decisions and sacrifices to keep all the parts in balance.

Key & Important Takeaways:

- There is more to happiness than money.
- Focusing only on the end goal can be a trap, but so can focusing only on the process.
- Happiness is not one thing—it's a combination of many different aspects of life that you keep in balance.

Self-Discipline Creates Balance

There's a quote from Ilona Mialik I always think about:
"Freedom without discipline is foolish; discipline without freedom is insanity."

It might seem counterintuitive, but self-discipline and happiness are more related than most people think. Most people think happiness is the freedom to do what they want. Still, the truth is we always have that freedom—and if we use it without any forethought, we might actually end up less happy than we started.

For example, take the freedom to go on the internet or social media in your spare time. It may seem like having the time to do that would make you happy, but I know people whose screen time goes beyond the hours they would spend at a full-time job. I've met people who work for 15 minutes, scroll social media for three hours and then work for another 15 minutes only to end exhausted and burnt out.

On the other hand, if you're living a life that's all work and no play, you have plenty of discipline, but you don't have any freedom or happiness. Sometimes we have to do work sprints or put in extra hours in certain circumstances, but we don't want to do it unless it's adding to our long-term goals—and we definitely don't want to do it all the time. On both sides of the formula, it's important to stay balanced.

A big part of staying balanced is self-discipline. In whatever it is you're doing, you need to build systems in your life that you can keep track of to know what's going on. That means balance in food, sleep and relaxation—everything needs to be accounted for in your routines and systems. No matter how much we want to be free and impulsive, human beings need structure. Without structure, we get chaos.

If you're juggling relationships, home life, schoolwork and whatever else, there's a good chance you're not taking time for yourself. That also means you're probably not getting time to think about what it is you really want and how to get there. If this sounds like you, you may be living out of balance. And getting back in balance is key to achieving your highest potential.

For one thing, we need to keep our inner life in balance through good habits—and there are plenty of ways to do this. On the one hand, you could take up a basic exercise habit to keep your brain and body healthy. If you're not exercising much now, but you want to, don't overthink this. Go for a short run every other day, lift some basic weights or start the day with some push-ups. Maybe you want to start the day with yoga instead—whatever it is doesn't matter. Just start the habit, and the system will begin to build itself.

Aside from that, don't focus only on your work at the expense of everything else. Even the most driven people need a mental break from time to time, so build this into your routine. Try starting a basic meditation practice for times throughout the day when you know you usually lose focus. This can be as short as five to 10 minutes whenever works for you—morning, afternoon or evening. On a bigger level, try to work in some basic self-care or rewards for when you achieve a big goal. Save up and go on a trip or a nice restaurant or buy yourself an Xbox. If you've been on a work sprint, promise not to work on the weekend for a few days and go to the beach to relax.

An easy way to think of it is in terms of a million-dollar sports can. If you had a million-dollar sports car, how would you treat it? Would you forget to get the oil changed? Would you use cheap gas? Would you store it outside where it could be affected by the elements? Generally, most people would say they would spare no expense or comfort taking care of the car —but the truth is *you* are the million-dollar car. How are you going to treat yourself?

Key & Important Takeaways:

- Self-discipline and happiness are more related than most people think.
- Without routines and structure, we get chaos—and chaos generally leads to unhappiness.
- How well you treat yourself determines how successful you will be to a large degree.

Become Your Own Authority on Happiness

Early in my life, I took advice from people I looked up to who I thought were authorities. Some of that advice came from entrepreneurs, parents and friends. Still, there's one thing I wished I knew earlier: some authorities are full of shit.

Even if your parents, your older brother, your teacher or your community leader mean well—even if they have success in their own life—it doesn't mean they will have the answers for you. Sometimes, you need to let people's advice go in one ear and go out the other.

Nobody else's map to happiness will work for you—everyone has their own experiences and their own passions that drive them. But more to the point: if you have a dream of running a million-dollar company, why would you let someone with a $40,000 salary talk you out of it? It's not that the person making that is less than anyone else; it's just that you need to appreciate the reality of the advice you get, particularly as a young entrepreneur.

Time and time again when I was growing up, my dreams were getting stepped on by people older than me who were the supposed authorities. No matter how many times I heard, "that's not realistic," I still made my first six figures at age 19—and now I have people in my network who spend that much on their jet fuel! Again, the point is not financial gain but the *impact*. Ultimately, having the financial resources available means you can make a bigger impact.

In my guidance counselor's eyes, she was right when she told me to give up on my business and that I wasn't going anywhere in life by not focusing harder on school; that was all she knew in her reality. From my perspective, I was watching 16-year-olds make millions online in weeks. In the internet age, there are no more boundaries, qualifications or borders anymore. There are always opportunities out there to make money if you're willing to learn.

When it comes to happiness and success, you have to dig deep and ask yourself why you're doing what you're doing. If you're in a career or relationship you don't like, or you want some new friends, take action to change those things—but also ask yourself questions. Why did you end up in those places in the first place? Why do you really not want to stay where you are? If we just take action and follow our impulses without thinking about what we're doing, we usually keep repeating the same patterns that keep us trapped.

In life, happiness is important because it drives everything else. If you want to achieve great things, you need to figure out what will make you happy about those things in order to get there—and it's a question only you can answer. Material success is not a guarantee of happiness, and anybody can be unhappy, but the other side of that is that you can learn to be happy wherever you are with whatever you have. After that, you can use that positive thinking to get to the next level.

Key & Important Takeaways:

- Even if the people around you mean well, it doesn't mean they have the right answers for you.
- Only you can draw your own map to happiness.
- You perform better when you're happy—so to achieve the greatest things possible, figure out what makes you happiest.

CHAPTER 4

FIND YOUR DRIVE

When I was about 15 or 16, I'd been in overdrive for too long, and I knew it was time for a change. I needed to refuel and cool down, or all sorts of engine lights would start going off. I had to turn some of the negativity I was feeling in being held back into fuel to push myself forward. I had learned enough, and I knew I could use my photography and team-building skills to launch my own agency.

To start, I went on Fiverr in its very early days and looked for people providing graphic design, copywriting and marketing services. After that, I would resell those services as a project manager. It was shocking to see how far behind businesses were when it came to marketing (and many of them still are). For me, marketing ideas had always been natural, unforced and smooth. I grasped onto the marketing and sales aspects quickly and decided to leverage that knowledge by going to business owners and telling them I could redo their branding, social media and graphics.

I knew I wanted to get into marketing, but I didn't have all the individual skills I needed. Even so, I knew where to look for the people who did have the skills, whether it was coding or design. I wasn't thinking of it in business terms at the time, but I was doing what any good CEO would do: putting together great teams to accomplish things that no one person could. At the same time, I was involved with organizations like the Boy Scouts and went to a National Youth Leadership Training summit one summer, all to hone my leadership and team-building skills.

No matter what other people were saying, I was starting to learn some real skills—and besides, I had never worried about fitting in anyway. I was used to doing things that were outside the norm if it gave me a greater chance at success, and this was no different. I was finding good vendors to work with and building a network, all while everyone else expected me to be nothing more than a student. While everyone else focused on their tests and schoolwork, I was daydreaming about how I could start my own businesses and follow my own passions rather than trying to memorize the same useless facts over and over again.

I was always doing a lot of things that weren't "normal." As a result, I got told no a lot. I remember when my grades were starting to slip, and I got put on the "at-risk" student lists, which basically meant we got "extra" attention. When I got called in by one of the academic counselors, she started asking me probing and loaded questions. "Is anything going on at home?" she asked. "Why are your grades starting to slip? What can we do to make sure you are on the right path to graduate and go to college?"

I was unfazed. The questions were turning into little more than force-fed advice. It was helping me realize that teachers weren't superheroes; they were just regular people with jobs and with their own lives. The counselor kept going around in circles and finally concluded the conversation with an ultima-tum. "If you don't stop focusing on your business and non-academic things, you will go nowhere," she said. "It will impact your ability to become successful at anything you want to do in the first place." I smiled and nodded, but I was infuriated by what I heard. The school had disrespected me—and they also removed me from any leadership I had, including clubs, the basketball team and anything else I wanted to be involved in. School was starting to become my enemy.

Key & Important Takeaways:

- When you've learned everything you can from a situation, don't be afraid to move on to the next thing.
- If you know what you're doing is important, ignore other people's opinions about it.
- Focusing on what really matters will usually lead to conflict—and you have to be prepared for it.

Start With What You Want to Do

As I became more successful at such a young age, I kept hearing one comment from people around me all the time: "Ishan, you're so driven!" As I kept climbing, it led to me hearing something else all the time, though now it was a question: "How can I find my drive?" In many cases, people talk about inner drive and motivation as if they're the same thing. The reality is they're not the same.

Motivation can be found anywhere in the world from any circumstances, but it's usually a fleeting thing. We *feel* motivated sometimes, and sometimes we don't. Motivation is nice when we have it, but we can't rely on it. It's a fleeting feeling that comes and goes. Drive, on the other hand, is a more powerful force than motivation. And the reason you can't "find" your drive is that it doesn't come from the outside. It comes from inside you.

You may be able to trigger yourself from the outside into getting motivated for a goal in the short term, but it tends to be a temporary high that goes as quickly as it comes. The real thing you're looking for is an inner drive that's like a steady flame that never goes out—no matter how hard the wind blows against it.

Another way to identify that inner drive is to take some advice from one of Mark Cuban's famous quotes:

"Work like there's someone working 24 hours a day to take everything away from you."

For me, my deepest drive and self-motivation began from wanting to do things differently than everyone else. When I was in school, even my teachers and friends were making fun of me for trying to start my own marketing company in high school. Even so, I never let other people telling me "no" get in my head or change my perspective on myself. Rather than being discouraged or talking down to myself, it only pushed me to do more and to go even harder. I wanted to prove everyone around me wrong. When people say "no" or put up resistance, I just want to push even further to get to the heart of the problem.

The deeper truth is that my drive doesn't come purely from wanting to prove people wrong. It comes from a deep love for the things that I *really want* to do. It comes from focusing on those things and making time for them rather than prioritizing what people tell me I *have to* do. Although they might not seem that different, that change in perspective is huge.

Key & Important Takeaways:

- Motivation is unreliable and fleeting; instead, focus on your drive.
- Your drive is the "why" underneath motivation.
- By knowing your drive, you can "trigger" yourself to push harder in tough situations.

Recognizing Your Baseline

Now that there are social media gurus everywhere, there's a big push that everyone needs to be hustling all the time and always being positive. We're getting sold an image of success that says the richest and most successful people never have bad calls or down days—they just push, push, push with a smile on their face the whole time. But we all know that's not what reality looks like.

No matter who your personal heroes are, I can guarantee that they go through all the same emotions as you do. What's even more important is that you don't have to be a naturally happy or optimistic person to be successful—and some of the people you admire are probably more pessimistic than they even let on. It's all about taking an assessment of who you are on a basic level and adjusting yourself to your environment based on your strengths and weaknesses. I call this recognizing your baseline.

The truth is you need to find your own emotional "average," and it's not the same for everyone. Jeff Bezos and Elon Musk have their own averages that are different than yours or mine. To figure it out, you have to ask some basic questions like:

- How do you usually feel?
- Do you tend to get angry very easily?
- Are you more light-hearted or serious?
- Are you more optimistic or pessimistic?
- Are you generally happy or generally stressed?
- What emotions do you least like to feel?

Identifying who you are on a basic emotional level can be helpful in analyzing the way you think. For some people, getting angry can distract them and push them into hasty, stupid decisions; for other people, a little anger is the perfect spark to push them to new heights. On the other hand, naturally optimistic people might be totally overwhelmed when they feel sadness, but someone else might have a huge tolerance for sadness, taking that energy and spinning it into an artistic masterpiece they can build a business around.

The point of answering these questions is just to paint a picture of how you usually are—and not because you have to change any of it. By writing these traits down on paper, you start the process of accepting yourself *as you actually are* instead of trying to change yourself or fit some mold. After getting that information, you can ask some additional questions about your processes like:

- When do you usually wake up?
- How long can you sit and work at a given time?
- How much do you like to eat?
- Can you focus better in quiet or noisy environments?

If you can recognize and observe how you process the world and how you deal with your emotions, you can maintain a lot more self-control in whatever it is you're doing. It means you can start designing your life and routines to cater to your strengths instead of trying to fit into environments that put you at a disadvantage. As a bonus, it can also give you a huge edge over people who haven't done the same inner work.

Before I figured out how to recognize my baseline and work with it, I was all over the place. I would get emotionally charged up when things didn't go my way, but I would also suppress my feelings rather than deal with them (like so many guys do). Still, even if we've been taught that having emotional spikes is a weakness, the truth is everyone gets happy and sad. Plenty of successful people have really high highs and low lows. It's part of the rollercoaster of life, and to stay on the tracks, you can't detach completely from your feelings as a way to be in control. Instead, you have to channel those emotions into productive things and use that energy for the good—even if it takes time to master.

As I was growing my new Fiverr-based business, I was going through a lot of growing pains in this area. Sometimes, the people I worked with would have friction with clients as a result of bad communication or logistics. Sometimes we would lose clients over it, and my immediate response was always to "punish" whoever I thought was at fault by getting angry. Over time, I saw that only made everyone's problems worse. Instead, I gradually started letting other people drive the conversation as I waited to see what was really happening.

I realized that often, you don't know what's causing people to act the way they are. You have your assumptions, but you don't really know. By choosing to listen first instead of react first, you can channel your frustration and anger into understanding and empathy, which is much more productive. There's a stereotype that the most successful executives are constantly firing people, flipping conference tables or throwing things out of 20-story windows, but that's totally inaccurate. The true masters of business know they can be frustrated and keep their cool.

If you recognize that your general baseline is slightly too low to get much done (or it's slightly too high, which makes you excitable and unfocused), it helps to figure out when this pattern is strongest during the day. Even if we have low energy levels generally, there's probably a time of day that we get a boost—and we should plan to accomplish our tough tasks during that time. If you're sluggish in the morning, it's probably not a good idea to pack all your tasks into the first few hours of the day.

Just as with strengths and weaknesses, optimistic people always see the best in others, and those who tend to be pessimistic can always see the downsides before anyone else. Neither one is good nor bad. Like anything in life, there are pros and cons for both sides.

The upside of a negative baseline is you might have an edge on problems or issues other people don't see, or you might be pushed to higher levels of quality than anyone else thought possible. In other words, if you're a perfectionist, it can mean you do really high-quality work at the expense of being at peace in your inner emotions. Out of balance, negativity can make you so critical that you lose drive and motivation—or it can demotivate people around you.

It's similar to the idea of "red teaming," which has been written about in several business books. In essence, it means you build a team of one or several people who are full-time devil's advocates in your company. They are people you hire to criticize things and give you the negative viewpoint when you tend to see everything positively—all to strengthen your skills and hone your execution. While too much negativity can drain you, a little bit of grit can also sharpen your blade.

If you tend to be pessimistic or negative or critical, look at where you're starting and what you can do to improve the things you can. Beyond that, start thinking about how your outlook gives you an edge and what other people value about you. If you're optimistic and positive, build some habits that help you harness that energy best without making you bounce off the walls or spin your wheels on problems.

Don't think that because your personality is a certain way, you're disqualified from being successful or achieving your dreams. There are a million different kinds of people in the world and so many different examples of success. Perhaps above all, remember that your perspective isn't fixed, and it can always change.

Key & Important Takeaways:

- Not everybody is (or should be) the same mentally or emotionally.
- Knowing how you usually think, feel and react is your emotional "baseline."
- No emotional baseline is right or wrong; there are always pros and cons.
- Use teams and routines to work with your baseline rather than against it.

Minimum and Maximum-Focused Perspectives

I noticed in high school that people tended to have a minimum-focused perspective (though high school also encouraged that kind of thinking). In other words, they looked at problems and asked: "What's the *minimum* amount I can do to get by or solve this problem?" A similar thing happens when we're minimum-focused in a social setting. Rather than looking up to people who inspire us with their accomplishments to model their behaviors, sometimes we negatively compare by thinking of ourselves as better while looking down on other people.

In any case, both of those perspectives will get you nowhere in life. They'll take you farther and farther away from your real inner drive.

To keep high levels of drive and motivation, it helps to spend time with people you look up to—and to have the self-confidence and strength to not let that intimidate you. Sometimes that means shifting your perspective so you can use your emotions for your own benefit. Instead of feeling like you have nothing to learn or that you're the best, open yourself up to being challenged by others and be inspired by what they do.

In many of the rooms I go in, everyone there is bigger or more established than I am in their own fields. It puts what I'm doing in perspective for me. When I'm there, my goal is not to copy other people or overly compare myself to them. The point is to absorb what they bring to the room and build off their skills and characteristics in a way I can use. When you're around people who are industry leaders or millionaires and billionaires, you realize success often comes down to how self-aware you are. Everything else flows from it: how good your timing is, knowing how to leverage your network, how quickly you can make decisions and so on. Because of all this, learning to find and embrace your competition is very important.

If you're in an environment where your friends and family are putting you down, or your teachers and mentors aren't guiding you, you tend to get detached. You get desensitized to your own goals. To stay on your path, you have to do whatever you can to find like-minded people who will boost you—whether it's signing up for a program near you or driving 15 minutes out of town to put yourself in a better environment. If you do this enough, it's a great way to make sure you're focused on the world around you and on real achievements rather than being so focused on yourself and your thoughts.

In my experience, finding a true drive and purpose means you have to progress through all the basic needs and yearn for something beyond them. It's not all or nothing—and you can see the progression by looking at Maslow's hierarchy of needs.

By looking at the pyramid, it's clear there are different levels of drive needed to do different things. Depending on where you are in life, you have different needs, and your drive comes from filling them. When you're at the bottom, you need food, shelter and clothes—these are called deficiency needs, and your fullest imagination may also be limited until you get them. They're not necessarily fulfilling, but they are necessary to survive.

Once you're past those, you start into your esteem needs of respect and achieving a higher purpose. While these aren't "necessary," they are much more personally and spiritually fulfilling than the lower needs—and once you think you've achieved all there is to achieve, that's usually when the real breakthrough comes.

When you're playing at the highest level, you're very concerned with abstract concepts of self-actualization and creativity—but plenty of people *could* be at that level if they could figure out their self-esteem needs first. Similarly, if you can't feel love and belonging yet, you can't advance to dealing with self-esteem, and you'll be trapped there. The scary thing is that society often judges people based on their wealth and not their impact. We idolize billionaires, but plenty of those people have serious self-esteem and love issues. Even so, we take their advice and worship them like gods without really knowing them. As a lot of people learn from experience, having the wrong purpose can be painful (and more often than not, having the wrong purpose comes from chasing something that is only external).

It's important to remember that wealth doesn't mean success. Real success is impact. Have those millionaires we're thinking of made the world better? Have they improved people's lives in a real way? Sometimes the answer is yes, but plenty of times it's no.

Above all, it's important to feel a connection to the things you're doing at a gut level. I use my gut to ignite my drive. Throughout my life, it's been my gut that put me in the rooms with people I needed to be around. It's that kind of drive that goes beyond motivation because it doesn't rely on your feelings that day.

I wouldn't be where I am today if I'd allowed myself to stay comfortable. I had to do the things I needed to do when I didn't want to, and you have to do the same. I noticed over time that even when it came to networking events, plenty of people would RSVP and then bail at the last second. It was like they were giving up before they even started. It's been said millions of times in other places, but just showing up consistently is so underrated as a path to success.

I told myself early on that even if I wasn't prepared or confident, I would still show up no matter what, even if I didn't feel like going. By doing so, I got ahead and was able to learn skills money couldn't buy—including soft skills like how to introduce myself to people, how to keep track of important business cards and how to hold your ground on important topics. They're things that are hard to teach, but that become second nature with practice and exposure.

Sometimes it meant that I looked pretty stupid, but I gained so much opportunity through it that it was all worth it. After all, if you don't put yourself in the environments you want to be in, you won't know what other people with the same interests are thinking. And if you don't know what those people think, you won't know where your skills fit into that conversation—and how to use them in a unique way that could become a back door for you to a happier and more fulfilled life.

It's easy to end up moving towards comfort—but comfort is a killer when it comes to growth and drive.

Key & Important Takeaways:

- Avoid people who ask: "What's the minimum I could do to get by?"
- Instead, find people who ask: "What is the maximum positive impact I could have?"
- Surrounding yourself with people you admire will inspire you and push you to go further.
- Even if these situations are uncomfortable, if you keep showing up to them, you will keep growing.

Avoiding "Shiny Object Syndrome"

Identifying and nurturing your drive is a challenge all its own, but maintaining it is just as difficult. Part of the reason it's so hard for young people especially is because of what I call "shiny object syndrome." To understand that, you have to

understand the cycle of emotions so many business leaders and
entrepreneurs go through on new projects:

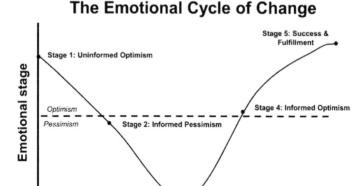

Whenever you start a new journey or goal, you're bound to
be excited about it at the beginning. As time goes on and things
slow down, you get irritated, and you start to lose your drive
and excitement. You start procrastinating and looking elsewhere for more excitement, and eventually, you might even
become totally uninterested in finishing at all. You're looking
for any kind of distraction to pull you off course, and at that
point, you start heading down the path of failure.

The way to think of this is that when you hit the bottom of
the curve, you start getting interested in new "uninformed opti-
mism" rather than seeing the thing through. When I was
starting my business, I fell victim to this as well.

I was running my photography company, a marketing
agency and trying to build an app all in the same three months.
The result was that I couldn't focus and wasn't making enough
headway on any one thing. I knew I liked variety and didn't

want to do the same thing all the time, so I decided to dig into the agency business. That way, I could help brands connect with customers, find new clients and solve new problems every day—all while still focusing on one core thing.

I've seen many young entrepreneurs be excited and focused on their goals when their project is new, but as soon as they see something flashy or distracting, they lose focus and start chasing that instead. They get pulled off course and end up going in circles.

It's just like what professional chefs go through when they stop being hungry for their own food. They've been in the kitchen all day, working hard and making delicious five-star quality meals, but because they've been smelling it all day, they're not hungry when it comes time to eat. Though it may not be such a big deal for chefs, that can be a huge problem in other contexts.

As a personal example, the book you're reading now was originally going to be called *Success by 18*. Then I got older, and it became *Success by 21*. Now I'm almost 22, and the title changed several more times before it was finally done!

We all have met people in life who had many unfinished projects, side businesses, new projects and so on. They are people with a lot of ideas but not enough execution. Whenever you get an idea or some motivation to do something, you have to own it, protect it and put it in motion right away for it to become real. And if you really care about it, you can't let anything get in your way.

This isn't just a problem that affects lazy or unfocused people—even high-level entrepreneurs can fall victim to it. Even Evan Britton, the founder of the website Famous Birthdays (which *The Atlantic* called "Wikipedia for Gen Z"), is a good example. Britton wanted to make money starting web-based businesses, but he soon saw a problem with his strategy: "I had a company where I owned a network of seven or

eight websites, and nothing was moving, nothing was growing....It was a lot of work to keep everything afloat, and it taught
me to focus. To actually succeed on the web, considering there's
such a low barrier to entry, it's really good to have a really great
niche. Everything was stable, but I wasn't making an impact."

Rather than keep pouring energy into everything equally,
Britton focused on being the go-to place for Gen Z influencer
and fan information—and since then, he's only been more and
more successful.

I've met a lot of people defined by money, but the truth is
that money should be a byproduct of doing what you love.
Chasing a dollar can quickly become a wild goose chase
because you can make money doing anything—mow lawns,
run a car wash, do phone screen repairs, start a housekeeping
service and so on. The question is: do you really enjoy the business you're running, and are you passionate about it? If you
chase that, you'll have a drive you can sustain in the long run. If
you chase money, you'll just end up becoming a slave to it.

To figure out what drives you, ask yourself what you could
do every day for the rest of your life. Does what you're doing
now excite you to the core? Is it something you can put your
name and your family's name on? Is it something you can
scale? If you follow the answers to those questions and go deep,
you'll push beyond surface motivation into a deep drive that
will sustain you for a lifetime. And when you find your drive, it
becomes that much easier to find back doors to the life you
really want.

Key & Important Takeaways:

- Motivation and drive go in cycles with both highs
  and lows.
- If you're in a slump, identify where you are in the
  cycle to reorient yourself.

- Being ambitious and having many ideas can be good, but don't "smell your own food" so much that you lose your appetite.
- To find your truest drive, ask yourself what you could do every day for the rest of your life.

CHAPTER 5

BREAK OUT OF THE COMFORT ZONE

Before my mentor Nick became a great photographer, he was a successful accountant. He was living the high life, making a ton of money and driving luxury cars. As I started learning from him in my own photography, it puzzled me at first why he decided to change careers. Over time, I learned that the answer was simple: he wanted to grow.

Instead of staying safe and complacent in a career he already knew, Nick listened to his inner drive. He'd always been passionate about photography, but there was a chance he wouldn't be as successful as he was in his current career if he switched. There was probably fear and doubt in the way. Even so, he pushed through it and decided to show up, again and again.

As he showed by example, showing up and putting yourself in the right rooms with the right people—even if it makes you uncomfortable—almost always leads to success. Nick knew that even if his skills and talent weren't fully formed yet, his attitude and willingness to learn would make up the difference. Without seeing what he did, it would've taken me way longer to meet some of the people I've had the privilege to meet. It all came down to getting out of my comfort zone.

For me, I discovered that photography was one of the world's biggest back doors to incredible networking opportunities. I could be standing at the most prestigious event in the world, but because I was holding a camera, people would walk right past me like I was invisible. It was the ultimate professional camouflage. It gave me the opportunity to rub shoulders with people who would've otherwise been totally out of my reach, all while they had their guard down. I did it at a young age, and it was a perfect opportunity to level up in life.

After seeing someone I admired, I could walk up to them when they were alone to strike up a conversation. "Hey, I took some great pictures of you at this event!" I would say. "I would love to send them to you directly because they're going to get lost otherwise—do you have a cell number or email I can send these to?" More often than not, these people wanted the photos, and immediately, I have the cell phone numbers of some of the most successful entrepreneurs in the world!

From photography, I learned how to be social, how to work a room and how to run my own invoices. I also learned situational awareness, including how to set the tone, move my equipment in and out and be part of any high-status room I was in. When I started my marketing company, I took those skills to networking events. Rather than trying to talk to people just anywhere, I could pull them aside to strategic parts of the room I knew were quieter and where we'd hear each other better. I'd also ask for things more smoothly as a result of experience I already had with my clients.

When I shifted from photography to marketing and consulting, I was surprised how much I could bring with me—I had built a foundation without even realizing it. As I started working with new mentors in marketing, some of the skills I already had helped me notice a difference between me and the older millennials I was working with.

As a Gen Z-er, social media and the internet were something I had my entire life. I was on social media forever, whereas millennials *got on* it at some point in their life. It wasn't their native language. Plenty of brands I worked with didn't know how to articulate what they did and how they did it online. They used generic imagery and stock photos on their websites, even if their company was pretty successful. I saw there was a huge market opportunity there that was virtually untouched—and though it mostly related to medium-sized businesses, in some cases it even extended to Fortune 500 companies! The result of taking all this in was that I turned all that busy work into strategic skills and success for myself.

I'm not saying everyone should do photography, but as my example shows, finding your own back doors starts with offering other people concrete value through the lens of your own skills. If you love to write, offer a small sample of your services to businesses you want to work with. If you're passionate about cooking, find events that wouldn't otherwise have great food service and offer your own services (and bring friends along to help). If you do what you're passionate about and creatively share those skills with others, there's no limit to how far you can go.

Key & Important Takeaways:

- You can't follow your deepest inner drive and stay safe at the same time.
- Following your drive and your passions helps you identify success shortcuts and "back doors."
- Finding your own back doors starts with offering other people concrete value.

Past Results Are No Guarantee of Future Returns

Humans are always looking for patterns, even if they're in

the past. Sometimes the patterns are based on data, and sometimes they're superstitions—like wearing a lucky pair of socks as a good luck charm for a pitch meeting or dribbling three times before making a shot in basketball. We're always looking for shortcuts and explanations for success, and we always want to point to something outside ourselves as the reason for it.

Part of that habit is reliving past successes and trying to duplicate them in the future (and when that doesn't work, we get frustrated and pissed off). It's why some entrepreneurs go from zero to 100 very quickly on one project but then hit a large speed bump on a new project, lose momentum and give up. They convince themselves that they're unable to top their past successes.

In my experience, the people who grow early on and then stop growing are typically the ones who start reading too many articles about themselves. They forget that they have to keep showing up and growing in new ways to be successful and become more focused on others' opinions instead.

In my marketing work, companies and individuals are judged on their most recent project, not on how successful they are overall. It means that you have to stay relevant and on top at all times. Every firm has its "lighthouse clients" who hold a lot of weight and shine to the rest of the world. It's great to have a few of them. Even so, the status they have doesn't automatically generate new business, and it doesn't translate into great work for a new client.

When I work with someone new, all the hard work starts over again from zero. It's my job to take it to the next level, which is a challenge I love to take on. It's what drives me forward. Even so, constantly having to start over and prove yourself again and again can inspire fear when you don't have much experience.

Fear might be useful in some situations (like the fear you feel while walking on the edge of a cliff in real life), but in many situations in the modern world, it isn't as useful anymore. The idea of losing a job or a client today is still scary, but the consequences are nowhere near as harsh today as they once were. Today, there are other options—you could apply for a new job, learn a new trade or start a side business. If you're young and you fail badly, you can often still move back in with your parents as a worst-case scenario. Thousands of years ago, losing a job or having a bad reputation in a small town could mean falling to the bottom of society automatically.

Sometimes our limiting beliefs come out of negative experiences we've had. I remember when I was in the fifth grade, I spent weeks preparing for a talent show where I was going to play piano. I'd practiced for weeks and had my music memorized. I was well-dressed and sat up straight and played the music by heart—I could've been blindfolded for how well prepared I was.

The experience I got out of it was positive. I felt the energy of the room and the people clapping for me. Still, if I hadn't prepared and the whole crowd had booed me off-stage, maybe I'd have more fear about public speaking today.

When you have a negative experience, it's like being thrown into the pool when you're really young before you're ready. The shock of it can make you afraid of water for the rest of your life —even though you don't have to be. No matter what the experience was in that moment, our brains trick us into replaying it again and again, overapplying it and holding us back from situations that aren't as dangerous as we think they are.

It reminds me of the Baader-Meinhof phenomenon, a cognitive bias where after you notice something once, you tend to think you're seeing it again and again in your environment— even though you may not be. We usually think of it in terms of someone mentioning a new movie to you, and then you see billboards for that movie everywhere, but it also applies when it comes to anxiety and negativity. If you're worried about a certain problem, you will find that problem and the conditions for it everywhere around you.

We bring these feelings with us as patterns anytime we experience something we don't have a definition for. We end up reliving bad memories without even realizing it. Fortunately, there's a way to take our control back, to unwire our brains and see everything as new again. It starts with a technique called Cognitive Behavioral Therapy (CBT).

Key & Important Takeaways:

- We always look for external patterns to explain away our success, but sometimes the only pattern is our effort.
- You can never redo old successes; you have to create new ones.
- Without examining them, negative experiences can keep us stuck and stop us from growing.

Rewiring Your Brain

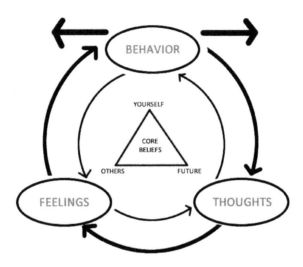

In the 1960s, psychiatrist Aaron T. Beck came up with CBT to treat patients who had persistent negative thoughts. He did this by uncovering the links between our behaviors, feelings and thoughts. Let's break those down:

Behavior: What we choose to do and the activities we're involved in.

Feelings: Our gut instincts and body-level impulses.

Thoughts: Our mental chatter and plans.

The basic rule behind CBT is simple: *The voice you hear in your head is not "you." You are more than the voice in your head.*

It makes sense to think of our behavior, feelings and thoughts in a constant feedback loop with one another—in both directions.

On the one hand, positive behaviors and actions lead to positive thoughts, which lead to positive feelings, which lead back around to more positive behavior. But it also goes the other way around. If we have negative thoughts about ourselves, it also increases our negative feelings, and those negative feelings affect our behavior.

The important thing to notice is this cycle works no matter where you start in the feedback loop. Still, while our feelings and thoughts often follow each other closely, they both follow our *behavior*. And shifting behavior can have a big effect on the rest of it.

As important as it is to "think positively" or "process feelings," that's hard to do and ultimately pretty useless without any action. If you think about how you're out of shape and then feel bad and worthless about it, often the next thing that happens is paralysis. You think badly, you feel bad and then your *behavior* is to find something to deal with how bad you feel and not necessarily to find something to help you improve. Instead, try to focus on thoughts and feelings from the angle of your behavior: *Do I eat as well as I could? Do I get enough exercise? What action can I take to shift this problem?*

To do this requires the skill of stopping this cycle midstream and realizing you are not your thoughts. Instead, we are our thoughts, our emotions *and* our behavior—and mostly, we are our behavior. For more intensive help with fears and phobias, you could work with a therapist who is CBT-certified. If going to a therapist would be too expensive, there are a ton of free tools, online worksheets and workbooks to help you practice CBT on your own.

The entire point of doing CBT is to reframe our experiences so that they don't control us for our whole life. When something bad or challenging happens to us, our body and brain have an instinct to react and encode it immediately. If a friend or a business partner lets us down, we spring into action with rationalizations and excuses—maybe it's our fault, maybe we're not good enough, maybe we deserve this, maybe this will keep happening and so on.

The important thing to know is that in these situations, we still have a choice on how to view it—but it's up to us to recognize that and to actually make the positive choice.

We can reframe our experiences. If someone lets us down, maybe it's because of something they have going on, and it has nothing to do with us. Maybe our actions or our plans were too intimidating for them to handle at that moment. Maybe there's nothing wrong with us at all. And maybe next time, the results will be more positive, and we should keep doing what we're doing already.

In all the above, time is an important factor. Even though these experiences happen in the present, they tend to pull us off-center and push us into the past or the future. We might go back to the past to all the other times we've been let down and add this to our imaginary folder of evidence. Then we shoot ahead to the future, adding more imaginary instances of being let down and disappointed. If we can keep our perspective and manage our emotions, we won't get pulled off course.

When we don't reframe our negative experiences so we can take action, we become our own biggest inhibitors to success. The way you get past it is to find a drill sergeant, either in your life or in your own head. Find a voice that will push you past your own boundaries to get wherever you need to be—and be prepared to hit road bumps along the way.

Key & Important Takeaways:

- Our behaviors, actions and thoughts are all connected—and often the voice in your head is not "you."
- Doing CBT can rewire our behaviors, actions and thoughts in a positive way.
- Without reframing negative experiences, we become our own biggest inhibitors to success.

Why The Comfort Zone is Overrated

The concept of a "comfort zone" has been talked about so much by this point that it's practically a cliché. Still, it pays to understand where it comes from and what it's for.

It's hard to track down who first came up with the concept, but it was repopularized in 2009 by Alasdair White, a British performance management consultant and theorist. As he writes in his book *From Comfort Zone to Performance Management*, the earliest written record of it he could find was from 1991 in a paper by Judith Bardwick.

Even if the origin of the concept can't be nailed down, it's relatively new even if we're all familiar with it. The comfort zone is the natural balance we get to in all areas of life where we're "cruising along." After learning some skills and achieving some level of mastery—in relationships, life or business—our minds want to stay at a certain plateau where we're not challenged because it makes our lives easier.

Our brain tells us to conserve energy and to work as efficiently as possible, so we start clinging to our current situation because we know it so well. Staying in the comfort zone can make us risk-averse. If we don't check ourselves, we might even start to think that what is around us is all we *can* get or all we deserve.

To put it simply: *that's dead wrong.* But to understand it better (and how to get out of it), you have to put the comfort zone in a bigger context.

When we're in our comfort zone, we're working on things we've already worked on and solving problems we've already solved. It's a safe place to be, and it's a place we get to after acquiring skills and mastering them. But for one thing, our comfort zone is not a fixed place. It's a reward we get for putting in a lot of practice—and it's a zone that can always change or expand.

Whatever the situation, once you realize you're comfortable, you tend to want to stop and rest. That's fine every once in a while, but when it becomes your entire lifestyle, it often comes at the expense of personal growth and deeper fulfillment.

If you're feeling stuck, it's important to find your own reset button. When you're stuck in your own negative loops, it feels like your motivation is gone and will never come back. It can happen through failure, from family members talking down on you or from procrastination, but it's something everyone has to deal with in some form.

As I've learned over time, what gets you from A to B doesn't necessarily get you from B to C. In other words, self-growth isn't always linear. When we master a new skill, it often feels like a breakthrough that pushes us to a new level of success. Still, once we get to that level, we need to experiment all over again to find out what will take us to the next level—which means there will be additional setbacks before the next leap forward.

Still, the key to finding the next thing that will lead to that breakthrough is to leave the comfort zone and see what's on the other side.

Key & Important Takeaways:

- Staying in the "comfort zone" is overrated.
- The comfort zone is not a fixed place; it's a reward for taking on challenges and can always expand.
- Anytime you feel stuck in one place, find a way to reset before pushing forward.

CHAPTER 6

MANAGE YOURSELF

I hate using notes when I'm giving a speech. It's my habit to be fluid and in the moment rather than rigid. When I have to read, I can freeze up and lose track of what I'm doing. It's why one presentation I was supposed to give was so nerve-wracking. I was getting ready to speak in front of 500 people—many of whom were older than me—about generational marketing strategies and how to reach younger consumers. Before I got to the venue, I was pumped up and ready to rock the crowd. Then right before I went up, the stage manager handed me a piece of paper with some writing to read introducing the next person. It was a good three paragraphs of tiny text about the person after me, our relationship and why they were so great. As soon as I got the paper, I froze.

"There's no way I can do this," I said, looking right in her eyes.

"You have to!" she said. I looked back down at the paper. It was clear I was in a fight, flight or freeze moment. I had that hollow feeling in my chest, the feeling of loss of control, ears ringing and panic. I had to get myself out of that state if I was going to go on stage—if I didn't, it would be self-sabotage. It's moments like these that make it clear just how important self-management is in all aspects of life.

Self-management has two sides to it. There's the physical side that includes things like having good routines and keeping track of data, but there's also the mental aspect and the health aspect. Good self-management can mean waking up at the same time, doing a morning routine and getting to work on time—but it can also mean being in touch with your emotions and regulating them well. To take that even further, it requires eating good food and taking care of your body—because your mind can only do so much if you're running your body into the ground.

To get started on all aspects, you have to get organized. This means creating daily, healthy routines and making systems for success. When you're not organized, you immediately become scattered and confused. Your energy goes in all directions instead of in one place.

The outer part of self-management begins with goal-setting —for that part, I have a simple tool I like to use. The first step is to create a statement that you want to see happen. For me, that statement is simple:

I want to create one of the world's best marketing companies.

Still, that statement isn't enough on its own—I need a plan to make that vision a reality. To do that, I break the statement down into three things that need to happen for it to come true. That looks like this:

1. I have to have a vast portfolio of clientele.

2. I have to work on projects that are cutting edge and viral.

3. I have to scale and grow my company.

Those become my core goals. Under each of those three points, you create three more points under each of those. Like below:

1. I have to have a vast portfolio of clients.

2. I have to take on clients that I know I can perform well for.

3. I have to continue to grow my brand through my work.

4. I have to diversify into different industries.

From there, you can keep doing this—keep breaking things down smaller and smaller until you have things you can do every month, every week and every day. I would tell you the rest of the plan for the marketing company, but I have to keep some of my secret recipe for myself. It's a good lesson to learn on your own—protect your goals and strategies like they're a secret formula because every time you say them out loud, they can get weaker.

The above is a good tool to keep yourself in check and to break up your complex goals into simple things that you can knock out one at a time. Doing so will keep you motivated and driven without losing track of the day-to-day.

Key & Important Takeaways:

- The key to self-management is organization.
- Both inner management of emotions and outer management of routines can help you succeed.
- To develop a long-term self-management strategy, start by setting goals.

The Art of Visualization

While goal-setting is good for making a plan of action, it's not always easy to motivate yourself simply by writing down a list of steps. This is where visualization comes in to bring your enthusiasm for your goals to life.

I like to think of visualization in terms of riding a motorcycle. When you picture someone driving a motorcycle, wherever they look on the road is where they end up going. If they look sideways, they go sideways—and if they can't see something, to them, it doesn't exist.

Whenever I set a goal, I picture myself at the finish line—not because I enjoy the finish, but because that way I can see what the final form of my visualization looks and feels like. For example, if my goal were to run a marathon, my first thought would be me ripping through the ribbon with everyone clapping around me, and then I would go into deeper detail. I would feel my ankles sore and my back aching; I would feel myself panting, out-of-breath with exhaustion but knowing it was all worth it. In essence, I would be replaying a made-up recording in my head of something I want to have done. Once I have that visualization, I reverse the clip—and then I do whatever it took to get to that part of the movie.

When you visualize the end product, you're manifesting it in your mind like it actually exists already. So many people do what it takes just to get to the finish line, which is why they fail. They didn't do enough visualization of what the entire journey looks like and what it takes to get through it. The finish only lasts for 20 minutes or so, but the journey can take years. To run 26.2 miles, you have to do it for hours, and you have to train months and years before that to get good enough! If you only picture the end and not the whole process, it's like you're skipping to the last pages in a book. You're setting yourself up for failure and a lack of fulfillment.

When I visualize, I try to picture the entire journey, not just the destination.

The most important thing when applying this way of thinking is to learn to enjoy the process. The process is where the entire story is made, and the end is just where the story finishes. So many people torture themselves day in and day out, only thinking about the ending of their goals and not actually enjoying the process. If you do that, you're going to miss out on a ton of enjoyment.

There's an entire world of people who make promises and commitments that they don't follow up on in real life. The issue is that there's a commitment problem there—but like anything else, there's a solution that can change your life when applied correctly. The reason why so many people fail at keeping their commitments is because they fail to communicate the importance of those commitments to themselves. More than words or images in your head, you have to turn the entire thing into a 3D reality in your head—and you have to fall in love with it ahead of time. Once you do that, you will start doing whatever it takes to get where you want to go.

Most people's instinct is to make a blanket statement promise to themselves that has little to no weight—things like "I'll get in better shape" or "I'll start my own business." Without any story or commitment behind it, those are hollow statements that will buckle under the slightest pressure. When you make a commitment, you have to be able to see it perfectly in your head along with all the steps it will take to get there.

For example, if you're committing to waking up at 8 am every day, put a ton of detail into that commitment. Think about how you'll be lying in bed and what the alarm will sound like in the morning. Then, think about the first few moments where you lift yourself out of bed and how you'll feel. What do you put on that morning? What do you do right after that in your morning routine? By doing this, you complete the entire task in your head before you even start.

The key to all of this is to fall in love with the commitment as much as the visualization, and it will always come to life, no matter how big or small. That's the kind of visualization that has to carry on into whatever you do. The only disclaimer is when you're let down, it hurts. Sometimes you don't rip the ribbon or make it to the finish—but that's okay. Failure is your best friend.

An exercise to put this into motion is to wake up every day and complete a routine. Knock that routine out, whether it's making your bed, doing 20 push-ups, taking a cold shower, whatever. Then, celebrate that small win of successfully completing that routine and starting your day off on the right foot. That kind of initial success sets a momentum of success in your goals that you can keep going on a day-by-day basis. Most people are in a position where they feel down and low, but they overlook the patterns in their life that keep them where they are. By focusing on the details and staying focused on small things, you can rack up lots of small wins and change your view and your momentum in a more positive direction.

Key & Important Takeaways:

- Before setting goals, use visualization to picture them already completed.
- While visualizing, communicate the importance of your commitments to yourself as clearly as possible.
- For visualization to work, you have to fall in love with whatever it is you're picturing.

Learn to "Service" Your Goals

A goal without a plan of execution or consistency won't take you where you want to go. Similarly, your goals can sometimes block your motivation if they aren't at least a little flexible. For example, turning down the opportunity of a lifetime at a huge company in favor of building your own company while you're still young might not be the best idea—maybe it makes sense to take the opportunity for a while for the experience and then return to your original plan.

Just like a car, sometimes your goals need a check-up—and once they're in place, you may find you need to "service" them from time to time.

Having goals that are too strict can be harmful, but so can having goals that are too loose. It's important to find goals that are realistic enough that you can achieve them but ambitious enough that you'll reach for them. Once you set a goal, it's your responsibility to get there—but the goal itself shouldn't crush you emotionally or be a distraction in your daily life.

If your goals are holding you back or frustrating you, it might be time to make an adjustment—and I've met people over the years (mainly peers my age) who struggle with this. When you're evaluating your goals, ask yourself these important questions:

- What have I done to contribute to what I want to achieve?
- Have I been consistent?
- In what ways have I failed?
- In what ways have I succeeded?
- What should I change in the next phase?
- What have I learned about myself through this process?

It can be excruciating to keep running uphill at the same speed. You're going to face all kinds of different slopes in life, paths you thought you would never take, complete with unfamiliar twists and bends. For those reasons, it's important to look back and cherish the distance you've come—and to use a map to see where you have to go next.

Key & Important Takeaways:

- If your goals are making your life unmanageable, you can "service" them.
- Without giving up the end you're picturing, adjust your timelines as necessary to avoid burnout.
- While pursuing big goals, track your habits and progress to keep adjusting and making progress.

Anxiety and Anchoring

Even with all your tools and systems in place, you may still run into situations where anxiety is threatening to take you over—like me with the paper before the speech. In those situations, it's easy for our self-management systems to break down, and then we fall down the dark rabbit hole of anxiety. Once you're there, things can escalate quickly.

If you were in school, that thinking would go something like this: I lost my pen, now I can't take notes! If I can't take notes, I can't study, and if I can't study, I'm going to fail! If I fail, I won't get a diploma, and without that, I won't get a job, and I'll be broke—I won't be able to pay for food, and I'll end up living on the streets, and I'll die! Though it seems like an exaggeration, there's no limit to the crazy negative loops we can go down over the smallest things if we're not careful.

Fortunately, there are techniques and systems for these panic attack scenarios too. One that I use that's very powerful is called anchoring. Anchoring is my way of hitting the reset button. You can do it anytime, anywhere, and if you keep practicing, it will become more and more useful as a tool. Doing it is pretty simple:

Right now, think of a moment that for you was pure happiness. It can be something from when you were five years old, and your parents got you a birthday gift, or it can be as recent as last week. It just has to be a moment you can truly relive, that you can feel in the moment. Once you have that moment, hold onto it and then put it aside.

Now, think about a funny moment. Maybe you watched your friend walk into a pole, or someone told a joke, and you laughed uncontrollably. Again, it should be something you can recreate in your mind and practically burst into laughter about. Once you've got it, lock it in and put it aside.

Next, think of a moment where you felt pure, raw confidence—that feeling that runs down your spine when you come in first in a race, or win a prize or have a crowd cheering for you. It could be something your parents congratulated you for or something you accomplished after a ton of hard work. Feel it, hold it, and put it aside.

These three moments or things are each equal pieces of your anchor. You can use a good anchor of three memories to completely reset yourself, no matter what state of mind you're in—but you have to do it correctly.

Now that you have those three thoughts, start switching between them quickly in whatever direction you want to go in. Cycle between your funny, happy and confident moments and keep doing it, over and over. Stay in each moment for two to three seconds before switching and cycling through them 15 to 20 times. Happy, funny, confident. Happy, funny, confident. Allow yourself to keep feeling those feelings and release your stress. When done correctly, you'll feel yourself emotionally reset.

The final part of this exercise is to "place" the anchor somewhere on your body. After you've cycled through those emotions, you could tap your wrist multiple times to anchor it there or tap the top of your head. As you do this, it'll cement that emotional charge back in your body in the present moment. If you practice this technique again and again, you'll be ready to take on the world.

Key & Important Takeaways:

- Without managing anxiety, it's easy to get caught in negative thoughts.
- Though everyone experiences anxiety, there are exercises to control it.
- By doing an anchoring exercise, you can change your emotional state and perform better.

Managing Stress Levels

Most people are familiar with that aching pain when something is going wrong or about to go wrong. It's stress, and no matter how much we're taught to accept it or work with it, too much stress can be very bad for your health—mental and physical.

Stress comes from a reaction to a perceived threat in an environment. When we see the threat, our brain fires off a signal from its emotional centers to the rest of the body. It's basically a neurochemical alarm system that we should be battle-ready—this means pumping our adrenaline, which increases our heart rate and elevates our blood pressure, and cortisol, which increases sugar in the bloodstream and makes the brain burn more glucose. Though this reaction might be just what we need if we were fighting off a grizzly bear, it's not the best thing to have over and over again when we're wondering if we'll have money for rent or if we'll hand work in on time.

In a stressful world, we need some good strategies to manage our stress. For me, it all starts with remembering that stress is just a temporary state of mind. Every negative thought and stressor has a beginning, middle and end. Rather than panicking over stress, remind yourself that it will end. So many people tend to get overwhelmed when stress piles up on them, which can lead to burnout, panic attacks and fight, flight or freeze reactions. None of those reactions are great when you have to solve problems.

To get control back and be proactive, it's important to acknowledge when you're stressed and to identify what's causing the situation. Ask yourself basic questions to get back in touch with reality:

- What's causing this?
- Why am I so stressed?
- What's the worst that will happen?
- Do I need to be so stressed to fix the problem?
- What do I need to vocalize to fix this issue?

Just asking these questions and running through this process might help you free up some mental space.

Throughout the day, all of us get dragged through life. Let's say every day we start at 100 percent. The first thing we do is wake up and grab our phones. We read the news a bit and go through our texts to see that one of our friends has said something negative, or an email popped up that isn't good news. We haven't even gotten out of bed yet, and now we're at 90 or 85 percent.

Next, you get up and head to the bathroom, thinking about what's ahead of you throughout the day, but you're still captivated by the negativity you just experienced. As you're lost in your thoughts, you start shaving your face or legs, and you push too deeply—now you have a cut. You haven't even left your house, and now you're at 75 percent.

Maybe after that, you look at the time and see you're running late. You rush out of the house, leaving things behind, grabbing your laptop you forgot to plug in the night before and the phone you left on the counter. Now you're at 50 percent.

To be clear, 50 percent is not enough to get you through the day. It's not enough to keep you happy. It's not enough for you to manage the issues that are about to come at you once you get to work—and if you follow this trend all the way through, a lot of the time, you get home from work, and you're at negative 50 percent. You're drained, and you feel stuck, broken, beaten and lost. You may even be confused as to how you feel as bad as you do, but if you break it down, it becomes clear.

Without a doubt, you have to protect yourself against stress from the second you wake up. Acknowledge whatever patterns occur that drain you of your energy, and then avoid or fix them. After all, doing the same thing again and again and hoping for different results is the definition of insanity—and you're not insane.

Stress is something I've dealt with in my own life—and not having good strategies only made it worse. The worst situations were when I was under a lot of stress and reacted by bottling it up and trying to push through it. I wouldn't communicate clearly with myself or open up with others, which ended up causing me to bottle up feelings until I couldn't hold them in anymore. I got into a place where I was reacting to life rather than responding to it—and when I look back now, I realize I should've just taken a breath. Thankfully, that's a pattern I've changed over time.

Some people use the words "reaction" and "response" interchangeably, but they're completely different. A reaction is instant. It's driven by beliefs, biases and pressure from the unconscious mind. You do it without thinking—it's something that just bubbles up automatically. When you react to things, you tend not to notice the long-term effects of whatever you did, which can create some devastating ripple effects. On the other hand, a response comes from a more conscious and well-considered place. You think about your emotions in the moment and about your goals in the long term.

For example, if you're approached by a panhandler and you give them money, why do you do it? If it's to avoid the conversation that's coming or to get out of the situation, it's a reaction. If it's to help them financially as a matter of personal principle, it's a response. Of course, these situations come up in business all the time.

One experience I had with these kinds of pressures was when I was late to turn in a client's project that had been due a week before. I was already feeling overwhelmed by tasks leading up to the due date, and the client reached out to ask for an update on where the project was. Instead of responding, I reacted. I told him I was busy and that I was working on it instead of thinking it through from his perspective. As a result, I gave a response that came off as disrespectful—it was along the lines of "it will get done when it gets done."

It ended up costing me the client down the road, but at that moment, I couldn't see the ripple effect coming. If I could go back, I wouldn't have said it. Instead of saying what I did, I could've said something like:

"I'm sorry for the delay. I've been overwhelmed with other work and had a bad start to the day, so I may come off a bit direct, but I guarantee you this project will be done, and my best people are working on it."

That response compared to the first one is so much better—and it could've saved me a client! As I've learned over time, words hold weight, and one word or sentence can change the entire course of our lives. Understanding how to process stress and not bringing that negativity into our communication is beyond important when it comes to being successful.

In many cases, a lot of us get beaten down by life and start to think that we have to take whatever we get without changing it. That's a mindset you can't afford. You have to protect your mental real estate as if it were the only thing you had—and it begins and ends with managing your stress levels.

Key & Important Takeaways:

- To face stress, begin by taking a step back from the situation and ask questions about it.
- If we're under too much stress, we don't respond to situations; we react to them.
- By protecting against unnecessary stress, we clear our mind to make better decisions.

Waking Up From Hypnosis

In a sense, we are always in a state of hypnosis. We're soaking in everything around us. If we're watching bad TV shows while scrolling Instagram and seeing sad posts and then we come home and someone gives us sad news, there's a high chance that we'll become very sad. We're being emotionally influenced by whatever environment we're in, and the same goes for the opposite—happy things send us to happy thoughts.

For these reasons, self-management relates to everything around you—and shielding yourself from negative influences is extremely important. To steer clear of negativity, once you've got good self-management systems in place, don't forget to celebrate your small wins. So often, we overlook the day-to-day and instead zoom out to the biggest possible picture. It's the same as when you do a zoom out on Google Maps and become a speck —when you zoom out to the planetary level, you barely exist.

The same thing can happen to us when we take on big projects that we think are beyond ourselves.

To fight back, we need to practice gratitude and stay focused on the moment. Focus on things like getting up and being grateful for a new day every day. Be thankful for having the ability to do whatever it is you do. Be thankful for the position you're in and for completing small projects that lead to bigger goals. As it turns out, reminding yourself to say you've done a good job for the little accomplishments is one of the hardest things an ambitious person can learn.

Key & Important Takeaways:

- Because of all the media around us, we are almost always in a state of hypnosis.
- Self-management and stress reduction are important to break out of that mental state.
- Gratitude and focusing on the moment are crucial to not being hypnotized.

CHAPTER 7

NOURISH YOUR RELATIONSHIPS

When I was younger, I didn't like to talk to people very much. I had good relationships with my close friends and family, but when I was at school or going about my business, I noticed a lot of people would tell me good morning or hello, and I didn't totally get it. Whenever it happened in public, it was usually with people I would probably never see again—what was the point of spending your own time to stop and engage?

I'd always been outgoing and ambitious towards my goals, but my relationships with people around me took a backseat. It was a trend that continued into my business life for a little while. When I was in meetings with people, sometimes I would just nod my head in interactions where I didn't think any more was needed from me. I didn't want to talk all that much—I was ready to get out of those interactions and onto the next big thing.

It wasn't until my friend Casey, another young entrepreneur, moved into my house that I saw there was a completely other way to be.

From the very beginning of knowing him, Casey was the friendliest and most outgoing person. He would say hello to everybody, and he would easily get socially sidetracked whenever there was interesting conversation to be had. Whenever I was in the backseat of an Uber with him, I was always wincing —I knew we were about to get the Uber driver's entire life story, and when the doors opened, it would be impossible to leave. In a lot of ways, Casey showed the opposite of my mindset. Where I was determined to focus on tasks and plans, Casey was always open to whatever might come up around him, and he always treated people like they were the best—no matter who they were. Although it didn't make sense to me at first, it was hard to deny that being around Casey was great. He made other people feel good, and he made you feel good by being around him. People saw him not just as an equal but as a friend—and his approach was getting him a lot of success in life and business.

What I learned from knowing Casey and being his friend was simple: everything in life is based on relationships.

Key & Important Takeaways:

- Being friendly and kind to others is just as important as hard work and accomplishing tasks.
- The key to the biggest successes is good relationships.

Kindness Is King

Everyone has heard the cliché "nice guys finish last," but a lot of people don't put it in the right context. Being nice isn't the same thing as being kind—and kind people definitely *don't* finish last.

In my world, being "nice" is not something that anybody should aspire to. Being nice means being middle-of-the-road or trying to avoid conflict with other people. It's making other people comfortable at the expense of your own comfort.

Being kind, on the other hand, means that you have a generous spirit. You are open to engaging with anybody and everybody. You look at things positively and constructively and you're willing to bring your full self into new situations. When you can help someone out, you help them—and when someone crosses one of your boundaries, you tell them honestly about it so they can improve. You're all about making connections with people and taking care of those connections. That's why being kind is the real path to success.

There are plenty of entrepreneur gurus out there on the internet who talk about getting big wins, always being competitive and hustling all the time. Though you need plenty of drive too, even entrepreneurs like Gary Vaynerchuk talk about how important kindness is—especially in influencer culture:

"You idiot influencers. You dream of having a life where you can do anything you want, when the reason that's possible is because people admire you and your content or how you make them feel. And then you go into the real world and they want to interact, and you try to act cool like you're somebody. Be nice. Kindness is the foundation of actual success."

Me with Gary Vaynerchuk (Entrepreneur)

Thinking of all those lessons, I was starting to consider Casey's advice. After I got some success in my business and through social media, I started to think more about my followers. I didn't want them to think I was just another guy out there who was cut off from them or unreachable. Instead, I followed Casey's example—I embraced them and opened up to them for feedback on all kinds of projects (including this book).

Though it's obvious by now, a lot of people in the influencer world are taught to be rude or ruthless and to push people away who look up to them or who can't do anything for them. But in the long term, that's a recipe for failure. Remember that when it comes to relationships and success. Your perspective shouldn't be about what you can take-it should be about what you can give.

I was recently at an event with my girlfriend. My original plan was to go there to support her, and I brought my camera to take pictures. What I didn't know was that there would be people at the event who would come up to me to ask for photos. I didn't know anything about who they were or what they wanted—but I was open to taking pictures with all of them all the same. Later on, I found out that many of them were major YouTubers—and as a result of being kind and open, I'd made a bunch of valuable new connections with them.

Carrying that same kindness and openness with you into all situations is so important because you never know who's around you and who you're talking to. Creating kindness is a good habit all on its own. It puts our focus on building long-term relationships and connections rather than on our own personal gain. It means not burning bridges with people, which is so important (because life is a lot longer than we tend to think).

There's an old saying that the people you meet on the way up are the same people you meet on the way down—and everyone goes through that cycle at some point in their lifetime. If you were kind to the people you met on the way up, they may help you bounce back up again when you're on the way down, but the opposite can also be true.

Key & Important Takeaways:

- Being "nice" isn't the same thing as being kind.
- Being ruthless or calculated can only take you so far.
- Creating kindness is a good habit all on its own.

The Right Boundaries Attract the Right People

At the end of the day, all relationships are imperfect. No matter how much we try to think of them in abstract terms, there's always a give and take, and everyone has their quirks. But all relationships should have boundaries—and being good at setting and enforcing them is an underrated key to success.

In professional relationships, we're usually talking about people we see at school or at work, people like bosses and coworkers. Usually, these are people you spend time with because of proximity or circumstance—you might not be willingly spending time with them, but you have to spend time with them. In your personal relationships and friendships, you have people you willingly spend time with. These relationships are non-transactional. It gets murky when these kinds of relationships overlap.

There are some people who view every relationship as a professional relationship. Even if that seems like it has advantages, in reality, it creates a very negative environment for people. These can be people who only work on building business connections at the expense of friendships or romance, or it can be people who treat their personal relationships only as transactions. These people usually struggle with communication and forming deep connections with people around them. Their relationships fall apart because they view everything as a transaction. People can sense that, and they stay away. After all, nobody who calls themselves your friend wants to feel like they're just a means to an end.

Even so, you can't treat every relationship like it's entirely personal and non-transactional either. In your friendships, you can't just give and give while the people around you take up your time and energy and don't help you in return—that's an example of setting bad boundaries. By the same token, just because a relationship is personal doesn't mean it's a true friendship. To put it simply, people can use you in personal relationships just as easily as they can in business.

I've met people who look at relationships all as one thing, no matter if they're professional or personal. To them, it's all the same playing field. The people who can successfully operate that way usually create complex and open dialogue with all kinds of people, and it ends up helping them grow. Still, not everyone can juggle all of that openness in all parts of their life.

For me, I like to keep my business and personal relationships separate. It helps me stay sane and lets me keep my head in the right place. It's important to have people in your life that you can open up to, but it's just as important to choose the right ones.

If you're struggling to find stability, it might be because your friends are unstable. If your friends are always asking you for things or pulling you away from what you care about, maybe they're not the best friends for you to have. If you feel like you're the most forward-thinking of your friends, ask yourself why that is. If that's the case, you may want to widen your group so that you'll be challenged more or that you'll get fresher insights. After all, the truth is your habits, patterns and behaviors end up being the average of the five people you spend the most time with.

In some cases, you may want to get out of relationships that are holding you back. The best way to do it is to be fully transparent and honest. The best way is to respectfully express your feelings to the people involved and the reasons why you want to go in another direction. Though it may mean a few minutes of discomfort and pain, that one conversation can save you from a lifetime of disaster. If there's someone who is a negative drain on your time, it's important to replace that energy with something else. Meet new people, learn something new or take up a new habit. If I've learned anything, it's that you can always replace bad habits and relationships for better ones with a little effort. Above all, you can't cling to fear, and you can't be afraid of hurting someone else at the expense of hurting yourself.

I've personally struggled with finding friends at times because for me, it's difficult to maintain relationships. I love connecting with people in different professional contexts, and I'm still in touch with people I met when I was 11 years old. Still, it feels like I have a lot of friends; the truth is I still have very few that I consider very close to me. The people in your inner circle are the ones who can disrupt your life or expand your ability to grow the most—and when you have a lot of projects you're working on, sometimes you have to keep that circle relatively small. After all, maintaining too many relationships can get overwhelming.

Key & Important Takeaways:

- All relationships are imperfect.
- Setting the right boundaries is key to keeping personal and professional relationships healthy.
- If your life feels particularly unstable, your relationships may play a role in that.

Connect with People—Any Age, Any Time, Anywhere

A lot of younger entrepreneurs have this thing where they get intimidated by older people. For whatever reason, we think of older generations like they're our parents and find it hard to approach them. If I could teach anything, it's that older entrepreneurs and business people are just like normal people—in fact, all people are just people. And there's no reason not to try to connect with anyone you're interested in talking to.

No matter what age gaps may exist between people, what really matters are shared interests and what we can bring to an interaction. Some of us may have been on Earth longer than others, but that doesn't mean you should be scared or careful around certain people. Although this sounds obvious, it's a major anxiety that a lot of younger people deal with.

In reality, we should look at our interactions with people in terms of what we can do for each other. There's no reason to be intimidated by an older person that's working on the same things as you or who is bringing value to a similar field in a different way. To look at it another way, that person is someone who may have lived two to three times as long as you have—and what they know about life and business can amplify whatever you have to bring to the table.

Me with Brian Cornell (CEO of Target), Mitchell Modell (Founder of Modell's Sporting Goods) and Michael Dart (Partner at Kearney)

I've been in plenty of rooms where the people there were all four times my age, but was I afraid to learn from them? No! Any time you're in that situation, you can get wisdom and information that might take you multiple lifetimes to learn on your own. I've found that in any situation like that around high-status people, that's a good way to look at things. Instead of seeing industry experts as direct competition, think of them as opportunities to get lightyears ahead of the crowd by learning from them.

Like every skill, getting comfortable in these different social settings takes practice. It's hard to push yourself, but the only way to get past it is to move through it directly. If you're nervous about being on the phone, spend more time on the phone! Stop texting and being on social media and start building those interpersonal skills. If you have extra time, watch videos on YouTube about how to network and demonstrate value to other people! There are hours and hours of free content on the internet, and there's no excuse not to take advantage of it.

Key & Important Takeaways:

- Young entrepreneurs have no need to be intimidated by older business people.
- Look at interactions with others in terms of what you can do for them, not vice versa.
- The only way to get comfortable in many different social situations is practice.

Deal With Egos With Social Intelligence

In business, you're likely to meet people who think of themselves as bigger than they really are—and you may also meet people who think they're smaller than they are (or you might think this about yourself). I've met people with huge egos who thought of themselves as greater than everyone around them, but by the same token, I've seen talented people who under-value themselves and keep getting taken advantage of as well.

Either situation can cause major issues in your relationships and your life.

One thing is for sure: if you're going to be successful in business and life, you'll likely have to deal with some big egos. And in that setting, it pays to know how to handle yourself. Out of heated discussions and arguments, sometimes great solutions and breakthroughs can happen for you and others. But in other cases, things can get off track, and the arguments can get personal and unproductive. In those situations, it's important to know at least a little bit about escalation and de-escalation.

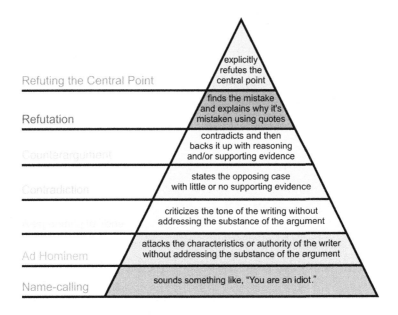

It never feels good to have our best thinking shot down, and there are a lot of different ways that it can happen. Even so, it's one thing to get clearly and directly told why our idea won't work, and it's another to have someone telling us we're stupid or hopeless. The same applies to us when we talk to other people.

The above diagram is an adaptation of Graham's Hierarchy

of Disagreement by author Paul Graham. Graham is an entrepreneur, computer scientist, venture capitalist and writer —and he's had to put all of these skills to use in creating his success. Without getting too technical, a lot of communication breaks down when people make their points from the bottom of the pyramid. The more we can talk to each other from a higher place, pointing towards deeper points, the better off everyone will be.

Learning business etiquette by honing your phone skills can be just as important—and you have to do it the same way. If you're shy, challenge yourself to meet new people every day. Make sure you have a good handshake and maintain eye contact throughout your interactions. Show interest and contribute rather than just listening to what the other person has to say. Finally, you don't always have to be talking to be engaging either—sometimes the power of silence says a lot more.

When I was younger, I was always outspoken and defiant. It gave me a strong voice, but I still needed to learn more about how to flow with conversations as I got older. Even if it sounds abstract, these are the kinds of valuable soft skills that they never teach you in school—but they're skills that you need no matter what you want to do.

In life, you have to communicate with all kinds of people. There's no way around that, so you have to make learning those skills a priority. If nothing else, a good starting point is to see everyone as equal. When you look at people as different from you—whether you think they're better or worse—they're going to feel you carrying the conversation differently, and it's going to cause separation.

When I started in entrepreneurship, I thought business people, celebrities and other successful people were like aliens. Deep down, I figured they must all just be a different breed of person which let them become so great. But as I spent more and more time around people, I realized just how untrue that was. Most of them are completely normal and approachable people, despite their success. The sooner you realize this, the better off you will be.

When I was a photographer, I looked at other photographers as competition, but I was still friendly with them. Other people would try to come up and connect with me, and even though I kept some distance from them, I never completely shut the door to connecting with them. They knew we were competitors, but they also knew that I wasn't a bad guy, and I was upfront in our communication. The funny thing is I later launched a marketing agency and ended up hiring a lot of those people I met. If I had totally been standoffish at first, it would've probably meant losing a lot of talented people later down the line.

As easy as it is to overthink social situations and friendships, the biggest thing I've learned is to keep things simple.

When it comes to relationships of any kind, being transparent and honest with your feelings is usually the best way to be.

Obviously, we're bound to act a little differently towards people when we need something from them, or we want them to like us—it's easy to be that way around millionaires and billionaires, for example. Even so, that mindset can be so detrimental in the long run. No matter what surface image a person gives off, there are plenty of people in high places who might not even know what the hell they're talking about. You have to evaluate people and advice on a case-by-case basis for yourself.

People who are honest and direct are powerful because they're so rare. When you embrace that, you become someone others can count on for real thoughts and real reads on situations, which is so much better than flattering people whose ideas you don't like.

When thinking about where we fit in the world around us, it's usually best to stop overthinking things and try to view everyone equally. Everyone is an opportunity in their own way, and you never know who will connect with who. There's no way to predict which people will prove helpful and beneficial and which ones will be negative. In social life, there are endless doors and opportunities. The important thing is to always be willing to connect—with anybody, anywhere. After all, you never know when you're going to meet someone again down the line.

Key & Important Takeaways:

- In business, being able to deal with others' big egos is a crucial skill.
- When dealing with conflict in business, focus on de-escalating in a professional way and don't get personal.
- Above all, balancing honesty and directness with professionalism will get you far.

Understand Your Family's Perspective

Throughout our life, the people who are around us the most are our core family—our parents, siblings, close cousins and whoever else. That support system can be invaluable in life, but it's important to realize that those people play a major role in shaping who we are. Even if we don't realize it, we tend to mimic and mirror our parents in our social skills and subconscious behaviors. These can be things that help or hurt us, but it's important to understand and recognize the patterns we pick up from them.

If our parents argue, we might internalize and repeat their same style of arguing. If they're always growing and teaching themselves new things, we might do the same. If they beat themselves up or are excessively negative, it will be a trait that we have to watch out for in ourselves. We're just extensions of our parents and our family systems—though it depends on how much time we spend with them, it's usually the case. And it's important to own our responsibility in those relationships.

It's important to understand where our parents are coming from, but it's important to understand our perspective. Without that, we won't understand who we are or who they are. For the most part, parents try to build the best lives for their kids. Still, they end up distorting reality to do that. When we're young, this can have a huge effect on us if we're not aware of it.

For example, your dad could be working countless hours before he finally comes home and gets some time to relax, and then he ignores you. He's not ignoring you because he doesn't love you; it's because he needs time to unwind—but we only see it from our perspective, which is just the tip of the iceberg.

Many times when our parents hurt us, it's because they're dealing with problems we're not open to. Latching on to hurts or wrongs can skew us off our path or make us take on things that aren't even our fault. In a bigger sense, the moral is to take time to understand other people's perspectives. If you understand where someone is coming from, you can help assess any situations that come up with them in a fair way.

Communication and time can fix almost all problems. When you have time away from a situation, it helps to give you a fresh perspective. You don't always have to fix things right away. Time and distance can be powerful assets when it comes to fixing relationships.

For the most part, whatever disagreements we have with our family come out of having different perspectives. Sometimes your parents want you to take a safer route, and you want to take risks and follow your dreams, which causes friction. On the other hand, sometimes we want something from our parents that they can't give and it leads to resentment.

All families have some of these issues. Communication, space and time are usually enough to get through them. If you're stuck in a bad cycle with your family, the best place to start is to acknowledge the situation for what it is. In an ideal world, you could get some distance to reset yourself or disrupt the pattern in a peaceful way. If you can't, ask to have an honest conversation to see how you could work together to improve things.

Key & Important Takeaways:

- Without realizing it, we pick up patterns of communication and habits from our family.
- Having unconventional or "big" dreams can put you at odds with your family—even if they mean well.
- When having a disagreement, you don't always have to fix it immediately.
- Taking time and space is important—after that, have an honest conversation on how you can improve things.

Take Space to Step Out of Negative Communication

When you're in the middle of a negative communication loop with someone, you can't see anything but what's right in front of you. Because of that, it's hard to judge correctly. Typically, the conflict is something coming from the outside that's triggering an internal feeling—like someone yelling at you, resulting in you being angry. Other times, it's an internal feeling only you have that's triggering a negative behavior—like someone tapping their foot and you snapping at them because you're irritated. Knowing the difference is important, and getting space can be helpful to determine what is really happening.

If it's an internal issue, where does it come from? Why do you get frustrated or annoyed at someone else's innocent behavior? Sometimes it's just a result of the way we're wired, but it's often linked to negative memories we have that we're not aware of. If it's the latter case, what memory or association is triggering you to be so upset? Without taking the time to recognize that, the same thing will keep happening over and over again, flipping you like a light switch.

As soon as your trigger gets hit, you have to be able to work backward from the trigger and unwire it. Without that clarity, you'll always be acting on the issue with distortion of some kind. When we make decisions impulsively from our emotions, it can lead to negative consequences that we didn't intend. To avoid that, we need strategies so that we can process things logically instead of emotionally. Here are a few ways to do that:

Think through the situation from the other person's perspective. It's easy for us to focus on our own feelings, but it's harder to think about other people's. To get around that, force yourself to explain the whole situation to yourself from the other person's point of view. Make sure you ask questions about why things are happening and what the other person is probably feeling in reaction to what you're doing. By doing this, we can get some distance from tough situations and make better decisions.

Look at the situation in another language. Though not everyone can do this, many people speak more than one language. If you do, one great strategy to get distance is to explain the situation to yourself slowly and rationally in a language other than your native tongue. Different languages have different nuances to them, and hearing it in a way that's unnatural to you will force you to look at things more objectively.

Do breathing exercises and keep a journal. For particularly emotional situations, slowing down and taking a few deep box breaths (inhaling for four seconds, holding for four seconds, exhaling for four seconds and holding for four seconds before repeating) can be helpful to recenter your nervous system. If you have a problem that is very complex and requires slow, careful thought, try journaling about it to get a little more clarity.

In all the above, the process is about identifying, distancing from and thinking through triggers. They can be positive triggers or negative ones—the goal is just to understand our wiring better overall to inform all of our decisions.

The brain is a sponge that absorbs everything, even if what we absorb isn't good for us. Ideally, we can use better communication and space to heal our relationships. If we need to cut ties with any bad relationships, we can still use these tools to help us see the way forward—and to help us pick who we want in our lives.

While self-mastery is important to a successful life, our relationships with other people can open more back doors than almost anything else. Even if we have great skills and talents, they don't mean much if we can't share them with the world. By improving your relationships and thinking of others, your life will expand more than you can imagine.

Key & Important Takeaways:

- Communication issues with others come from internal and external issues.
- To have interactions, identify your own triggers and look at the situation from another perspective.
- While self-mastery is important, our relationships can open more back doors than almost anything else.

PART II

BUSINESS

"Here's to the crazy ones, the misfits, the rebels, the troublemakers, the round pegs in the square holes . . . the ones who see things differently. They're not fond of rules, and they have no respect for the status quo....You can quote them, disagree with them, glorify or vilify them, but the only thing you can't do is ignore them because they change things....They push the human race forward, and while some may see them as the crazy ones, we see genius, because the people who are crazy enough to think that they can change the world, are the ones who do."

-Steve Jobs

CHAPTER 8

THE TRUTH ABOUT MENTORS

In the business world, it's getting more and more popular to talk about the importance of mentors. Anyone who's interested in entrepreneurship has probably read a blog post somewhere about how you need to find a mentor, develop an amazing relationship with them, learn all they know and soar to the top. But the concept of mentorship has been taken a little bit out of context lately.

To me, a mentor is simply a leader, and a leader is someone who's willing to do what they're telling other people to do. By that definition, there are potential mentors all around you! So many up-and-coming entrepreneurs think they need to have Mark Zuckerberg or any A-list celebrity name on speed dial to have a great mentor. Some of those people are great at what they do, but choosing mentors based on how much clout they have isn't a good strategy. Instead, find people who really lead by example, who you respect and who are experts in a given area you want to learn about.

That's the important thing that always gets left out: you don't need to put all your chips on one huge name to get the benefits of mentorship. One of the biggest things to understand is that mentorship is basically just fancy advice that comes from different people with different life experiences, and all that advice can be drastically different. That's why I truly believe finding people who are the best at any given thing is so important. You find someone who has built a system you identify with, and then you learn from them. After all, you wouldn't try to learn design from someone who specializes in Facebook Ads—you can find different mentors for different areas.

When you're looking for mentors, there are a few important things to understand. The first is that your best mentors might already be in your circle and all you need to do is strengthen your relationships with them. The second is that you need to know who you're talking to, what their experience and expertise are and what you want to learn from them. Finally, you need to understand that advice from experts is still just advice —and if you have multiple mentors, you'll need to consider all of it and make up your mind for yourself.

Key & Important Takeaways:

- The concept of mentors has been taken out of context in recent years.
- Mentors are just leaders you respect, and they can come from anywhere around you.
- You don't have to learn everything from one mentor —you can have many.

How To Pick (and Keep) Mentors

For me, finding mentors came down to looking for people I knew who were the best at what they did. They didn't have to be the best in the world. They just had to be the best I *knew*. The second key factor was that I never counted on one person to teach me everything, and I tried not to go to anybody who was wearing too many hats at once. It's better to have more mentors in a few focused areas than to have one mentor for everything who doesn't have time to help you learn.

A mentor doesn't have to be a genius. The key is to find people who live to a standard you're proud of or that you look up to. Good mentors are people with ideals and morals you would like to beat. Looking up to a modestly successful mentor who has a great family and a kid is in some ways a better mentor than a billionaire who has terrible relationships with everyone and is depressed.

Because a mentor will have a huge effect on your life, you have to look past their financial success and into their deeper aspects as a person—their health, wealth, love and happiness. As cheesy as it may sound, those are the four pillars you should screen for. Mentors can be balanced in all of those areas or be particularly good in one or two of them. Ultimately, it's all about balance.

You don't need to find someone who is perfect; in general, the people who pose as know-it-alls don't know left from right when it really matters. Instead, just find people who you respect and can learn from—and once you have people like that in your life, it's your job to keep them around.

You need to make it worth your mentors' time to teach you by engaging them, showing initiative and being willing to learn. Make it clear that you can be coachable and that you'll always give the relationship your all. Because mentors get a charge from teaching someone with a lot of energy and enthusiasm, become that person—and make sure you stay creative when you're adding value to whatever projects your mentor is working on. I learned that lesson early on.

My mentor, Diana S. Zimmerman and I.

With one of my first mentors, I would often come to her and simply state problems I'd found, which she didn't appreciate. "Don't come up to me with a problem prematurely," she said. "A problem is not a developed thought. A potential solution is a developed thought." It was a lesson that stuck with me.

Only come to your mentor when you have a full view of the situation, a potential solution in mind and a game plan about what to say. So many of us already have problems in life with no solutions, but why ponder problems without thinking them through? When we do that, we end up with negative thought loops and get stuck. We're married to our problems, but in reality, problems are temporary and are usually avoidable or fixable if you put in the effort.

Key & Important Takeaways:

- Mentors don't have to be geniuses or millionaires to be the right person for you to learn from.
- To keep mentors, be engaged and show initiative—but keep your own boundaries as well.
- Never come to a mentor with a problem without presenting a possible solution.

Avoiding Mentors Who Will Drain You

In my experience, if you stripped many millionaires and billionaires of their money and made them start fresh, they wouldn't be able to repeat their success. Some people get rich by innovating, creating new things and adding value out of nothing, but there are plenty of people out there who inherited money, got lucky or are running businesses that don't provide any real value to the world. Unfortunately, those are often the same people who want to give advice to everyone else from 30,000 feet up in the air. They are precisely the kinds of mentors you want to avoid.

I would rather take advice from someone who is in an industry I'm interested in than a billionaire who got rich off an idea they had 20 years ago. You have to understand that even if someone has a lot of credibility, they can still be a waste of your time. You have to develop a good filter for people to be able to choose the right mentors, and there are a few things I tend to screen for:

Filtering out the "lottery winners." Sometimes people's successes are more a result of good luck than good ideas and contributions. You wouldn't want to take advice on personal finance from someone who won the lottery, for example. Even though that's an extreme example, there are so many more instances of that in the world around us. When people are born successful or they have a few good ideas, get rich and never contribute anything again, they often don't have the right advice and perspective to give.

The internet is turning into a world where anyone can become "successful," but they're actually surrounded by a circus of bullshit. Many online entrepreneurs' only income is selling educational products about things they barely even understand. It wastes everyone's time and money—I've seen it again and again. That's why it's so important to do your research.

Look at what other people say about them and look at what they do every day. Look at what their personal lives around them are like. How does that person treat their employees? When I see people mistreat their team daily, I consider it a major red flag. How would that person treat you on their worst day?

Forget the showboats. When you see people who run around flexing all the time and it's all they do, they either have a personality issue or their ego is out of control. In other cases, maybe they're compensating for what's not there.

When evaluating people like this, look out for words that are buzzy or fluffy—especially anybody who talks about how good they are or says "I'm the best." Most of the true experts I know are very humble. If you met them on the street, you might think they were a schoolteacher or an average Joe, but behind the scenes, they're running a multibillion-dollar empire.

We often fall prey to people who are really good at talking and showing off. I've learned this through my own experience. Through my network, I've met people in high-status circles who throw parties where experts in different areas can mingle. I met someone through a mentor of mine who said he was a high-end developer and coder—this person had basically fooled my mentor into letting him into his circle as well. My mentor then put me in touch with this person, and because I trusted my mentor, I trusted the developer as well.

From that meeting, I put the developer in front of my own clients I was working with and paid him an advance. Shortly afterward, he took the money I'd fronted him and left me on the hook for work he wasn't able to deliver himself. All of it made me and my business look bad—all because I'd fallen victim to a con artist. Even though I lost the money I gave him, I think of it as paying for an important lesson: always do your homework and avoid the show-offs.

Always listen to your gut. Although people can add up on paper in a lot of different ways, it's important to trust your own instincts and needs when you meet people as well. Even if the person you're talking to seems impressive on the surface, pay attention if you get bad feelings about them. Don't fall victim to marketing and buzzwords. To get past the hype, you might have to spend some time seeing someone in action—in other words, seeing their real life.

Find someone who has a good routine and good relationships. I've been around people who seem successful on the surface and might come off that way to others when in reality, their inner life is worse than someone who has nothing. It goes back to the same point that whoever you surround yourself with, you become. Just as we pick up on the habits of our parents and friends, we also pick up on our mentors' behaviors and habits. Make sure you're looking up to the right people.

Be kind, but don't be too "nice." It's important to be respectful and enthusiastic when someone's mentoring you, but don't fall into the trap of being a pushover or not having your own opinions. When you're too nice, people can take advantage of you—and you don't want that to happen when you're on the way up.

When you're starting out, you're likely to find people who want to use you for your ideas, your excitement and your enthusiasm. From experience, I've been in environments where I put in 100 percent and ended up getting -50 percent back. It's not a good place to be, and it's important to set expectations and know why you're in the relationships you're in. In all relationships, you have to learn to keep a balance. **Use mentors only to go forward, not backward.** Ultimately, the usual idea we have of a singular mentor who is amazing at everything isn't as important as it once was because you can learn things anywhere these days. You can pick up a book and find expert information, or you can get online and watch YouTube videos to learn almost any skill. Even so, mentors are great to help you connect with people and get real-life experiences. Maybe the most important thing to remember is that mentorship doesn't have to be so formal.

I have people in my life that I provide free services for, and in return, they help me whenever I need it—and that works out well when one hour of their help is worth 60 hours of me trying to do it myself! Those are the kind of situations that are most beneficial to everyone involved—anywhere you can find huge efficiencies like that. Learn to see mentors as the fast-forward button to learning. Because if you find the wrong people, they can be like hitting the reverse button on all your hard work.

Key & Important Takeaways:

- Wealth isn't a reliable indicator of how good of a teacher a mentor will be.
- Aside from their business skills, mentors should be balanced in other areas like life and happiness.
- Be sure to pick mentors who will help you grow, not mentors who will harm your self-esteem or set you back.

CHAPTER 9

IDEATION

So much of what makes a business successful is the focus and energy a person puts in and their willingness to follow through. A lot of times, less successful people get overly focused on having a good idea rather than working hard or building a good team—which is a surefire recipe for failure and burnout. Ideation is important once you already have a successful business running, but most people want advice on how to find an idea to get them started.

For this, my advice might sound counterintuitive: don't try to be the next Amazon or Uber.

Am I saying that you shouldn't try to be as successful as you can be or that you shouldn't try to change the world of business? Absolutely not. What I'm saying is that when Amazon and Uber started, they didn't know what Amazon and Uber would grow into or become. Instead, they were built on simple ideas, executed well and ideated on as more success came over time.

To boil it all the way down, the questions you need to ask when getting started are what are my skills, and how can I build a team around them—that's it! Many people are under the false impression that they need to have a genius, world-changing concept nobody ever thought of before to get started in business. The truth is you just need skills and a team.

At the former Team 10 house with my client the Super Bowl Selfie Kid and others

Starting a business and growing it to profitability is harder in a lot of ways than working a job. You are creating something out of nothing rather than adding to something that already exists. Most startups and small businesses fail. To give yourself the absolute highest chance of success, doesn't it make sense to build your business around something you're really good at? Even if it sounds obvious, so many people try to come up with business ideas based on skills they don't have.

The best place to get started with ideation is to find something you know you're good at and then find a way to make money from it in the smoothest, most painless way possible. Once you've proven you can do that on a small scale, you can gradually and organically grow from it and learn new skills to spread your influence.

Key & Important Takeaways:

- If you're trying to start a business, don't try to be the next Uber or Amazon right away.
- To begin, ask yourself: What are my skills, and how can I build a team around them?
- Prove you can do what you're good at on a small scale; after that, you can expand.

Your Most Valuable Asset

After you've done those two things above, the next most important thing is how you're creating value from your skills and for your team. For 99 percent of people, they trade time for money, and that's how they price their services and products—and that includes entrepreneurs who supposedly don't think of themselves like 9-to-5 wage workers. The best way to run a successful business is to find a model where you don't trade time for money. Instead, you sell value and empower your team to make decisions to take yourself out of the business so it can grow on its own. In that way, the business model will generate recurring revenue so that your time gets freed up more and more, and your business runs itself to some degree. When you have those things in balance, that to me is true success.

People forget it easily, but time is the most valuable asset we have. If you want to make me go crazy, just put me in bumper-to-bumper traffic—I go through every emotion imaginable! In general, I'll always pay a toll to get my time back, which is the same reason why I don't have patience for people who waste my time.

To get started thinking about what you could build a business around, it's good to think of what I call *energizers and depleters*. To understand what I mean, it means thinking of things from the perspective of the energy they bring. As an activity for this, get a green pen and a red pen and make two lists. On the left are your energizers in green, and on the right are your depleters in red.

In each one, write the things you love and the things you're good at on the left. Some examples of energizers could be exercising, eating well or doing activities you love. On the right, put things you would rather not do—things like writing up proposals, drafting invoices, being struck in traffic and so on. This is an exercise you can do from a personal development standpoint or from a business development standpoint. It helps you understand what makes you happy and what doesn't.

By doing this, you will have a new perspective on what gets you going that goes beyond a simple pros and cons comparison. Instead, it's about the core things you're passionate about—and the things you can't stand. This way, when you're ready to build a business, you make your responsibilities be all the things in the left column. For the right column, design your life so that you can hire someone else to take care of those responsibilities.

Although this is a powerful tool, the one thing to remember is that I know some people who outsource absolutely everything—but if their entire team left, their business would come crashing down. The lesson there is that you should at least have some knowledge of the things that need to be done if you're going to avoid doing them yourself, so it doesn't all come apart at once if someone leaves.

Key & Important Takeaways:

- Always remember that time is your most valuable asset.
- To be truly successful in business, you should trade value for money, not time for money.
- Build a business around things that energize you, not things that deplete you.

Ideating Throughout Roadblocks

Once you have a good idea, ideation doesn't stop. When you're faced with a difficult client or a business challenge you haven't done before, you will need to keep coming up with new ideas and approaches as new obstacles present themselves. For these reasons and others, it is so important to understand the fundamentals of how a business operates before you jump into running one on your own. Often, these are lessons you end up learning the hard way.

When I was 15 or 16, I learned about some of these skills when I was approached by someone to become a part of their business. The person told me I would be selling a product but that he would have to introduce me to someone else to learn more about the sales process and how the business worked. Although it sounded good at first, I realized I was getting passed down the line to different people while getting sucked deeper into their organization—but I still wasn't even clear on how their business worked (or how I would make money from it). Nowadays, this happens to countless young entrepreneurs: they get approached by a multi-level marketing scheme.

Fortunately, I didn't spend very long in that funnel before getting out of it, but it did teach me one valuable thing: the power of credibility hand-offs. The idea is simple: Person A wants to sell something to Person B, but they know there will be a lot of resistance if they come in with a hard sale. Instead of doing that, Person A tells Person B that they *have* to meet Person C because meeting them will change their life—then they can proceed with business. Once Person B meets Person C, it's Person C who presents the hard sale (or in some cases, they pass Person B down to Person D). Though it might be put to scammy use in MLMs, the idea behind it is powerful, and it has applications for businesses of any size.

In essence, that "passing off" of responsibilities, duties and sales creates a powerful network around a potential customer or client. It adds a level of credibility and community to something that would be transactional otherwise. Every single new introduction is a kind of credibility fulcrum that lowers people's guard against the sale. Everyone knows that a good sale shouldn't feel like a sale; it should feel natural, the product should actually be useful, and the client should want it. All the same, this kind of "hand-off" technique can be used on hard projects to keep ideation flowing and to build up your clients' confidence in your process.

As I've learned time and time again, understanding communication is fundamental to dealing with struggles that come up on big projects. In hard situations, you learn that how you say things is just as important (if not more important) as what you say. When you've presented a set of designs or photos to a client and they immediately reject all of them and are frustrated or angry, how you react and communicate will affect how well you can ideate past that problem. If you suddenly get angry or defensive, things will grind to a halt. If you find a way to take in their feedback, explain your reasoning and offer to bring someone in to help push the project forward, you will be able to overcome virtually any problem.

In essence, making sure you can keep ideation going boils down to communicating well enough to protect that part of the process. Really, your communication with clients is just another part of sales—once someone is sold on your product or service, you have to keep selling them on your ability to execute it and on your processes. For that reason, it's not about mastering one message or one technique. It's about communicating your messages in an environment where they will survive *with a given client.*

Key & Important Takeaways:

- In great businesses, ideation never stops and is a major part of all processes.
- Ideation depends on communication, and how you say things is just as important as what you say.
- When working with clients, ideation can be another form of sales.

The Eight Clients Every Business Gets—And How to Manage Them

It follows from all the above that one of the first things you have to do when you're working with other people is to manage their expectations—even when you're starting out.

Everyone knows the pressure of needing to impress someone when you first meet them or the feeling that you're lucky to have someone ask to work with you, so you should do whatever they say. In some rare situations, you may have to bend over backward more than you like because it's unavoidable. Still, whenever you can, you shouldn't promise the world —keep their expectations reasonable and be transparent about your process. If possible, underpromise wherever you can (and then plan to overdeliver later, which is way better than the reverse).

There are certain "types" of clients who seem to come up again and again—and sometimes clients be multiple versions of these types throughout one project. Here are some guidelines to help prepare you to deal with them:

The Unrealistic Client

"Hey, I want this to be big and revolutionary. This all has to be done by next month, so we need to move quickly."

This type of client is often a visionary who comes to you with lots of big ideas and expectations. The biggest obstacle in dealing with them is understanding what parts of their vision are reasonable and feasible within the constraints of timeline and budget.

To address their lofty goals, start with a road map. Set a timeline of goals and projects and set firm parameters on what can be accomplished within your given parameters. It's important to validate the big ideas but ask, "Can we do this?" with our limitations to keep the focus on the attainable.

The VIP

"I decided to hire you for this, but don't let me down because I can take my business elsewhere. I will pay for everything once the work is done."

This is the client who is always holding it over your head that they "could hire someone else" if you don't live up to their expectations. While every client is important, the VIP wants to be placed above all others. They tend to position themselves in a way that demands your entire focus, which is most apparent in their frequent, often repetitive and unnecessary communications (which typically come with the expectation of an immediate reply). These are the clients who make you feel like you are always on the edge of losing their business if you don't meet their high standards.

To deal with them, find a way to demonstrate that your client is a priority while still setting boundaries and leaving space for your personal life and your other projects. By setting specific touchpoints with the client early on, you can acknowledge the importance of their project without letting it overwhelm you. These specific appointments also set the appropriate timeframe for client contacts. If all else fails, be prepared to walk away from these clients if they continue to make you feel inferior and don't value your role.

The Micromanager

"Hey (just) checking in to make sure everything is going well. I texted you last night and haven't heard back."
If you're an expert in your field, you get hired to do a job that someone else cannot complete themselves. A micromanager has a hard time acknowledging that distinction. They will try to stay on top of you throughout the entire process, often questioning tiny details, checking your work against their own experts and wanting near-constant updates. These kinds of clients are notoriously hard to satisfy because they hang onto every detail from start to finish.

Much like the VIP, it's important to set boundaries. Establish early on that you are the expert and that your purpose is to take their vision and run with it in ways that they cannot. Instill confidence and trust with set checkpoints. While it's important to hear them out, it's equally important to remember that you are there for a reason.

The Urgent Client

"Can we get this all done ASAP? It's extremely important because I have to submit everything by the end of the week and can't miss the deadline."
Some projects genuinely need to get done fast, but the urgent client is a rebel without a cause. They want it done right away—even if there is no justification for the speed. Often, an urgent client's demands involve sacrificing weekends or evenings and can often disappear after submission. This all results in a compromise of quality just for the sake of meeting some artificial deadline.

The fix in these situations is to ask a simple question: what's the rush? Find out from the beginning if this is a matter of true urgency or client impatience. If there's no real fire to put out, assure the client that you can create both quality and efficiency with just a little extra time. From there, create a deadline that meets everyone's needs.

The NYSMNYD Client (Now You See Me, Now You Don't)

"Hey, sorry, I haven't been on my phone. Let's jump on a call as soon as we can, and I'll take care of the invoice by today."

These clients can be tricky to detect since the NYCMNYD can often be mistaken for the urgent client upon first glance. Instead, these are clients who appear enthusiastic and ready to work out of the gate, only to disappear when questions arise or reviews are needed. They will often reach out absentmindedly without a clear grasp of where the project is because of their disappearance. Be warned: if not handled properly, the NYCMNYD can easily turn into a postponer with delayed calls and meetings turning into confusion and missed deadlines.

As with the others, it is important to set expectations clearly and in writing from the beginning with clients like these (and with all clients). A contract can often be the key to keeping everyone on task and at the table. When contact between the two of you starts waning, reaffirm that the timeline established is important to their success. It's also important to keep in mind that, while it's important to follow up, you don't need to waste your time chasing them down. Your time is equally important.

The "Yes, No, Maybe" Client

"I think this is a good option, but I feel like it can be even better, but I am not sure how I feel. What are your thoughts?"

Decisions, decisions. The "yes, no, maybe" client will

struggle with them all. They may try to rely on you to make all decisions, or they may feel the need to get third and fourth opinions, leading to delays and loss of direction. They also struggle with focus and will not offer feedback when needed. This can lead to mid-project directional changes, extended deadlines or dissatisfaction with the final product.

In general, these clients need a gentle but firm hand steering them in the right direction. Find a focus quickly, and keep written records to help prevent changes midstream. It's important to have a clear "why" for decisions to help prevent wavering. Don't be afraid to say no to last-minute course reversals that don't make sense. Follow up at clear milestones and interact at the end of each one to ensure everyone is on the same page and on task. More than any other, these clients need you to show your expertise to create a successful working relationship and final product.

The "Behind the Times" and "Viral Sensation" Clients

"We've done it this way for the last 20 years; can we keep it the same?" or *"I have a bunch of ideas to make us go viral!"*

These two clients are on polar opposite ends of the spectrum, but they come from a very similar place. The "behind the times" client wants to stick with what they know. They describe themselves as "traditional" and are resistant to innovation. The "viral sensation" client has the opposite problem. They want to jump on every trend, latching on to a meme or viral video and attempting to stretch their brand to fit in a box where it doesn't belong. They envision an impossible outcome with a strategy that really doesn't fit their company or goals.

While it may be counter-intuitive, both of these clients need the same thing: YOU. Explaining the "why" behind your techniques is important to push the traditionalists out of their comfort zone and to bring the virals back down to reality. Set the direction away from fads with focused content and an expert vision.

The Grasshopper

"That's great, but have you ever thought about doing this instead...?"

The grasshopper is a hard client to pin down. They hop from one idea to the next without structure. You may find yourself struggling to bring them to the table. Dialing the project into one point of focus can be even more of a challenge. "On task" is not in this client's vocabulary.

For these individuals, you'll need to provide the structure to reach their desired goals. It's a good idea to write down all of your questions and points of discussion in advance to avoid missing any crucial points during frequent topic changes.

All of the above will affect your approach to ideation in your work process, but all of the above can be addressed with good communication and by managing expectations. If you set their expectations high, you have to manage them—and that's on you! If you promise something to close a sale, you will have to face it and deliver it. In reality, you shouldn't try to close clients that you won't be able to keep or satisfy throughout your process. While there's no way one way to manage everyone's egos and keep things on track, one key part of it is to get everything on paper as soon as possible. That way, there can be no ambiguity in what's happening next and no hurt feelings if promises don't get met.

Key & Important Takeaways:

- Often, clients fall into one of a handful of "types."
- Though each one presents challenges, all of them can be managed if you set expectations.
- No matter the client, it's important for the business to set the tone and control the rhythm of the process.

Protect Your Ideas

Finally, when you come up with new ideas and strategies, make sure they're fully developed and fully baked before you go screaming them to the world. It's similar to the idea of the pro chef who smells his own food too often. The more familiar people are with an idea you have, the less prestige and value it will have in their eyes.

The same goes for goals and plans to achieve things. If you have a great plan for how to get what you want or how to execute your plan, write it down—but don't feel like you need to tell everyone else. The most important thing is to actually execute the steps you've visualized and planned for yourself, not to brag about how great things will be when they're finally done.

In my own experience, the more I talked about a project before it was ready for public consumption, the more likely it was that the idea wouldn't actually come to fruition. One early example of this for me was with domain names. Over the years, I must've bought more than 500 different domains on GoDaddy and similar websites for projects I had in the works before anything major had been done on the projects. My focus was on many different places at once. In some cases, I was going about things in the wrong order and talking up ideas that I hadn't executed yet.

There needs to be a balance between your ideation process and how well you execute. On the positive side, you're only ever one move away from doing something brilliant, and ideation is the key to unlocking the move. But once you've got it unlocked, the ideation process should stop. At that point, the most important thing is to follow through.

Key & Important Takeaways:

- When you have good ideas, be careful about sharing them too early.
- Ideas are fragile at the beginning and become less prestigious and exciting the more they get passed around.
- By focusing on good execution before sharing a project with the world, you help the original idea retain its value.

CHAPTER 10

MARKETING AND BRANDING FIRST

Sales and marketing are closely related, but almost everyone sucks at marketing. Marketing is the precursor to sales, and without it, sales don't happen. Usually, when you're marketing something, or you're being marketed to, all of the materials are pointing towards a click funnel with a monetization system put in place behind it. Even for a free online form as simple as entering an email, all those emails are being collected in an online database somewhere—and those databases can be sold for thousands or millions of dollars sometimes (depending on how many emails they contain).

To talk about marketing and branding, you have to talk about the old and new school definitions of it. According to the AMA Dictionary of Business and Management, marketing is:

"activity, set of institutions and processes for creating, communicating, delivering and exchanging offerings that have value for customers, clients, partners and society at large."

They define brand as:

"Name, term, design, symbol or feature that identifies a seller's goods and services as distinct from other sellers."

Both of these definitions are technically correct, but they aren't my definitions—and they aren't the definitions the new wave of entrepreneurs is going to associate with those words. To me, marketing is the entire experience and relationship someone has with a person, company or brand. Marketing is having the ability to put an image or experience in someone's head that you're trying to put there. It can be as simple as something that brings them a feeling of nostalgia, something that makes them curious or even something that provokes them. It's my go-to explanation for anyone trying to understand it: it's about the relationship you have with the customer and the idea in their head.

Branding and marketing go hand-in-hand. As a whole, branding is all of the images and aesthetics around the experience you want to push. A good brand creates a full experience out of something simple—it could be as basic as buying a water bottle.

When you go to the grocery store, there's an entire aisle full of different brands of water bottles, and they're all selling exactly the same product. There's nothing particularly special about the product itself, and there are not many ways to innovate the product or add on to it (when it comes to plain water without flavors, still versus sparkling is about as diverse as it gets). Even so, everyone has a favorite water bottle company, and they have an experience with it. When they pick it up off the shelf, it opens a mental tab in their head that says: "Oh yeah! I love this company." It's still just a water bottle, but a relationship has been created there.

When it comes to branding, if you can't articulate from a

written and visual standpoint what the experience is you're trying to create, your brand isn't marketing itself correctly. If marketing is the story you're telling, the branding is the actual sensory part of it—mostly the visuals, but sometimes the sound, smell and taste. A brand is walking into the W Hotel and smelling the sharp but smooth fragrance of flowers and a clean fall smell in the air. If you had a blindfold on, you would still know you were at the W Hotel.

People tend to think branding stops at the logo or the design, but branding is forever evolving—and it must evolve with a brand's growth. There are always new and better ways to position a product or service from an experience and design standpoint. Hopefully, companies can get better and better at that. Even so, plenty of huge companies don't even know where to start in this area.

Lots of companies look at marketing as something they have to do after a product is out or something that they have to maintain to keep up sales. It's an older way of thinking that ultimately the product or service is king and everything else is secondary. I disagree for a simple reason: if you have a bad product or service, but you have amazing marketing and branding, your product will sell. The same is not true the other way around. It's as simple as that.

For me, marketing is the backbone of all sales, and it leads to cascading effects. If you have bad marketing, then you likely also have bad sales; and if you have bad sales, you have bad distribution. If you have bad distribution, you have a bad customer experience. It's so important to think about marketing and branding almost immediately instead of trying to figure it out after because, in the new digital age, it's getting more important every day.

Key & Important Takeaways:

- Marketing is creating an entire experience and story around a product for a customer.
- If marketing is the story and experience, branding is the sensory details.
- Without good marketing and branding, good sales can't happen.
- In many cases, marketing should come before a product because it is upstream of everything.

Cracking the Back Door of a Branding Session

There are plenty of opportunities for young entrepreneurs to become project managers, designers, copywriters or even digital agency leaders in the current business context. In the case of so many older companies (or companies run by or targeting an older demographic), the world around them has changed, but their messaging, story and strategy haven't kept up. Their voice is coming across like some kind of Frankenstein monster on social media. In most cases, a company with bad marketing and branding is like if you tried to make a cohesive, finished puzzle out of six different puzzles. The parts don't go together, so the result is always going to be a mess.

Brands like the ones described above are constantly looking to younger entrepreneurs for guidance and understanding here, and they're hiring branding agencies to fix those audience disconnects. Because of that, it's good to know how these meetings can go and what you should be thinking about when you sit down in one of them.

Whenever I sit down with a company or brand, the first thing I try to get a handle on is the personalities of the owners. Who are they? Why are they doing what they do? What are their motivations? It could be "save the sea turtles," "better the planet," "make money" or "be the next Tony Stark." The specifics don't really matter; it just matters that you know them.

As a marketer, the important thing is to understand what that energy is very quickly and clearly because you can't turn a company with mad scientists at the helm and an edgy CEO into a flat, bland and overly professional package. The result would be almost cartoonish. Even so, there are plenty of major branding agencies out there that don't understand that. They can move into a company, design things and make it all look good, but when they move out, there's a huge disconnect between the materials that are being sent out to the public and the conversations being held within the company itself. It cuts all the way through product design to marketing emails.

To get started with any client, no matter how big or small, you have to understand the *why*. It's the soul of the company and the business, so you have to get it to its very core. Once you have that, you can extract a list of company values from that core identity, values that need to be expressed and that the audience has to understand. Just like with ideation, branding and marketing aren't always about coming up with the weirdest, most out-of-left-field idea. The most effective marketing and branding ideas are completely organic, growing specifically out of the client or company you're working with.

Because the best marketing has to come from a very pure, focused place, the first meeting is important. Getting all the right people in the room is crucial, and depending on the company, that includes very few people or a handful. From my team, the same thing is true. I like to have my design head and chief of staff in those first meetings with me, so we're all on the same page, but we can also scale up or scale down depending on how big the project is. The important thing is that there aren't too many hands on deck, tugging the ideas in every direction. Of course, these are strategies that every agency will have to figure out on their own with practice.

By now, Goel Strategies has built more than 50 brand sites for people and different companies, and we've learned a lot in the process. One of the funniest things that has come from it is that what the client imagines the work should look like in their head isn't necessarily the best thing for the brand—and that can cause friction. Again and again, it's important to stress that the marketing and branding are built for the *customers*, not for the owner. Even if bigger companies want to brand themselves to satisfy the owners, thinking about the customer funnel is crucial, and it begins with some simple questions:

- What will the customer see first?
- When and where will they scroll?
- What fonts would they like?
- What distances should the objects on the page be from each other?
- How can you make it visually appealing?
- How can you make customers stay on the site?

There are plenty of examples of CEOs and CMOs who have tried to build something they think looks and feels good, but it was a total miss with the clients. That's why it's so important to keep a fresh perspective.

I painted a lot when I was younger, and sometimes I would flip my paintings upside down and look at them that way. I had my initial idea of how the paint should go on the canvas and how it should be hung, but inverting it gave me a new perspective and allowed me to consider new things. I try to apply that same thought process today when it comes to branding—and it's particularly helpful with big clients and rebrands.

Key & Important Takeaways:

- A good brand requires a coherent and consistent voice across multiple platforms.
- To create a great brand, first understand the personalities of the people running the company.
- Brand stories should be for the customer, not for the people who own the company.

The Right and Wrong Way to Rebrand

There are plenty of big companies out there who have had the same branding forever. Sometimes a logo or a visual concept is so iconic, a company doesn't want to let go of it—and sometimes that makes sense. For a company like Coca-Cola or McDonald's, the core of their branding is so powerful that it's universal, and they don't want to mess with a good thing. Still, companies that don't have that same level of recognition or sales often rebrand to keep up with the times—but there are right and wrong ways to do it. To illustrate, think about these two examples.

One company I worked with was a startup in the fintech space. They had a small but passionate following of fans online, and their top leadership had successes with other businesses that had changed the world. Still, the top guys were charming and funny in person, but they were also eccentric and a bit brash in their dealings with the press and at conferences. Everyone on the team knew they had an awesome product that could disrupt the competitors in their market, but they had a problem that many people had: nobody really knew about them, and they had led with the product first.

Even though their product was great, the result of the mixed personalities on their team and the lack of focus on marketing meant there was no unified voice. They were saying one thing on their website, something else in live conferences and something else on social media. Meanwhile, each one had its own branding ideas that were all slightly different and not synchronized—and because of international finance laws, messaging about who could use their product and where was unclear. They had customers, but they were floating around, unsure of what was going to happen next. It was the definition of a Frankenstein monster when it came to branding.

For them, rebranding made a lot of sense—they had a great product that was a little confusing and no central voice explaining the story and experience to customers. After working with them, my team spoke to their leadership, understood their vision and created a message that they could use on all of their different platforms. We created a new visual style for them that was sleek, approachable and that explained the value they offered in the simplest terms anyone could understand. They were a textbook candidate for a strategic rebrand that we carried out to the fullest, but there are other examples where it doesn't make sense.

With the company above, we were taking a relatively new product that had an old-fashioned approach to marketing themselves and bringing it into the present. Still, around the same time, there was another company I worked with in the telecommunications space that was unrolling their own rebrand.

The company had been around since the early days of the internet, and their branding was wacky and edgy. It stood out from its competitors, and it told a story, all on top of having a great product. When they released their rebrand, all that personality disappeared. The new image had brought them into the present, but it had smoothed out everything interesting about the brand that had been there before. Now, they looked like one of a dozen other companies—even if their appearance was sleek and smooth.

OH no Type Co
@OHnoTypeCo

EVERYBODY FALL IN LINE!

4:45 PM · Feb 13, 2018

♡ 19.1K   ○ 6.6K   𝒮 Copy link to Tweet

The point is a company's branding and marketing have to be unique to who they are and what they do. A rebrand isn't just about fitting in with the times or looking like everyone else. It's about positioning yourself the right way for whatever environment you're in—but it's a fine line that's easy to lose sight of.

Key & Important Takeaways:

- For established companies, rebranding can be powerful or very harmful.
- A successful rebrand unifies the company's messaging and positions them for new audiences.
- A bad rebrand tries to chase the latest trends at the expense of a company's voice and personality.

The Harsh Truth About Creating Experiences

The unfortunate truth of it all is that very few brands can

create real experiences for their customers. Being number one in a given arena isn't enough these days, particularly as marketing experiences and technology change so quickly.

Again and again, I've been preaching experience as the most important part of marketing—and after years of saying it, the prediction is finally coming true. Even bigger brands are finally pivoting towards making the experience of buying and receiving things a priority, which means spending a lot of time on their website and packaging. It's all part of what it means to make an experience for someone: it's not just the product itself, and it's not just catchy writing or pictures. It's the entire story of finding the site, buying the product, opening it, using it and connecting with a community of users. It's putting the entire package together. There are plenty of big companies that still aren't doing these things (which means there are still lots of opportunities for marketing entrepreneurs to get in).

Ultimately, good marketing is about articulating culture and voice through the lens of a brand, but doing it in a way that is memorable and original—not something people will forget about. It's telling stories that become a part of people's day and a part of their life rather than just a piece of their day or a passing distraction. Marketing takes time to master, but becoming aware of it is a good first step because it's all around us. After all, you reading this book to this point is just another example of marketing and branding done right.

Key & Important Takeaways:

- The harsh truth is few companies can create real experiences for customers through their marketing.
- In the future, marketing will be even more interactive and immersive than it is now.
- The key to successful marketing is to become a part of a person's day or life rather than a distraction.

Brand and Market Yourself

Gen Zers have grown up on the internet, so they know more than almost anyone about TikTok, Snapchat and YouTube. All of those are great things to know about, but there are still other areas young professionals should look to position themselves for success as early as possible. There are social media sites and public platforms that are more for entertainment and some geared towards business. It's the second category that younger entrepreneurs could use more of.

Even if the topic of branding and marketing doesn't apply to you in a company sense, it applies to *everybody* in a personal sense. Business is moving more and more online, and the impression you make there can open doors for you. That's why it makes sense to bring a younger point of view to the places that business leaders and executives are looking for them and where there aren't many people who are experts yet. I tell every young entrepreneur I know to build their LinkedIn pages and to start answering questions on Quora. Even if it seems unusual, those are places major companies look for talent and personality, and it's where a younger perspective is needed the most.

People tend to devalue themselves and their contributions. The school system is partially to blame here for making us focus so much on fitting into a rubric or a box, which is the opposite of true creativity. The whole goal is to make employees instead of leaders or employees instead of people who can change the world. Many of us grew up tested on memorizing dates, filling out lists and regurgitating vocabulary words, but those aren't the life skills you need. What you really need is to recognize your own strengths, package them and sell them to the rest of the world.

Time and time again, I've seen huge companies take even one small idea from a younger person and completely change their business for the better—and I've also seen huge companies ignore their younger talent's ideas and suffer for it. All of this proves one thing: your skills and your perspective are valuable, but you have to recognize them first. And once you recognize them, you have to shout about them as loud as you can to anyone who will listen.

Key & Important Takeaways:

- Gen Zers have a marketing advantage because they grew up on the internet.
- To brand themselves better, they can focus on business-first platforms like LinkedIn instead of just social-first platforms like Snapchat.
- School teaches people to devalue their contributions, but Gen Z has valuable insights for the business world.

CHAPTER 11

NETWORK LIKE A BILLIONAIRE

The first time I met Mark Cuban was at the American Airlines Center in Dallas. I was shooting photos for Hoosiers Meet Mavericks, a night for new students accepted into the Kelley School of Business at Indiana University. There were a ton of people packed into an auditorium, many of them about my age. As a famous and successful IU alum, Mark was the keynote speaker. After his speech was over, he went downstairs, and everyone got front row seats to watch a basketball game—the entire thing was basically an ad campaign for the university.

Nick, my mentor, had been hired to shoot the event, and he'd brought me along with him. When the game was over, about 80 people were crammed into a box suite, all shaking hands and introducing themselves. Mark was the center of the energy in the room, but he was also giving it back to everybody—remembering names, shaking hands, making jokes and laughing loudly. He looked so comfortable in a room full of people who were all trying to impress him.

I knew it was my opportunity to meet Mark Cuban, so I stepped up. Every 30 seconds, someone was jumping up to get a picture with Mark—and as a photographer, it was a perfect opportunity to get close enough for a conversation. I was glued to him the whole night, and after the event, I tried the networking trick I always used: that I had lots of great pictures I could send him.

"Thanks, but I have plenty of pictures of myself," he said. I would have to find another way in. I kept telling him about how I'd worked with his brother Brian and that I knew other people at his companies, which made him a little more excited. Since I already had my foot in the door, eventually I was able to get his email. Later, I knew I would send him an email to follow up—it was too great of an email to pass up. Still, what are you supposed to write in your first email to Mark Cuban?

I wasn't sure what to write in there, and right away, the email was filled with dialogue and was constantly asking for reassurances—it was practically the same length as this book! I wasn't confident he was going to respond to me, and to cope with that, I overcompensated by over-explaining and covering every possible base imaginable. After I sent it, I waited around for a few weeks for a response. Unfortunately, none came.

I realized later that I'd ended up screwing myself over by waffling so much—who's got the time to read a book-long email? Definitely not Mark Cuban. With that in mind, I tried emailing again a month later with a much shorter follow-up that was just a few sentences. Sure enough, he wrote back almost immediately! Because I pushed forward, I eventually got hired by the Dallas Mavericks through a client of a client. It all taught me that by following my passion, putting myself out there and staying true to who I was, networking would start falling into place on its own.

*First time meeting Mark Cuban when I was hired to photograph an event
at the American Airlines Center in Dallas, Texas.*

Key & Important Takeaways:

- When networking, always establish a way for follow-up contact.
- In follow-ups, be direct and don't waste the other person's time seeking validation.
- By networking and following up, many "back door" opportunities will open up to you.

Overcoming Your Networking Fears

There are a lot of people who don't like the idea of networking; maybe they're hesitant to do it, or they don't know how. It's understandable to need a few tips since it can be intimidating, but building a positive network around you is of utmost importance. The greatest successes in life aren't built only on your individual skills. They're not built because you have a lot of money or because you have a lot of things. The thing that produces the biggest wins of all is being in the room with the right people at the right time. Your network is your most important asset.

It may sound controversial, but if you think about it, it's obviously true. It takes time to perfect a skill set, start a business, position yourself, save money and invest it to grow your wealth to the point where you have wealth and are respected in your field—but imagine if after all that work, you had to start over entirely. What would you do to rebuild if everything went away? If you build everything you have with a you against the world mentality, you'll be out of luck if it ever disappears. Still, if someone takes away all your money but you still have a strong network around you, with a little luck and hard work, you'll likely be back to where you started in much less time.

In my early experiences with photography, I saw the power that being in the right room had. I watched and documented all the connections influential people were making right in front of me, and I positioned myself to be a part of their world as well. After years of work experience and building my own name for myself, I'm now bumping shoulders with world-class speakers, presidential candidates, presidents, millionaires and even billionaires—people who impact millions of people. It's an important aspect of success that everyone should pay attention to.

Key & Important Takeaways:

- Networking is a common fear people have, so it requires reframing.
- Life's greatest successes aren't built on individual skills; they're built by teams and networks.
- A good network will help you rebuild from scratch much faster than just individual skills ever will.

Connecting Authentically with Other People

People often say things like, "I hate networking; it feels fake to me." The issue in those cases is that they're thinking of it the wrong way because their own self-image is off, and the way they're viewing the world might be off as well. When people come to events to meet other influencers or leaders in their field, they're not doing it just to take advantage or to take *anything* from the room. They're doing it because they have something to *give*. They're offering value to a room full of people who also offer a ton of value, and they're building connections with one another so they can offer even more value in the future. The issue comes when you're in a room with people like that, and you feel like you don't belong there.

Another word for it is "imposter syndrome," and everyone struggles with it at some point in their lives. Without getting too anxious or stuck in your own head, the best way to take action to get out of that headspace is to perfect your own image by making it as authentic to you as possible—it's the same thing I do when I work with companies on their branding.

To understand what your image is or should be, you have to understand who you are first. Are you loud, chaotic and in people's faces? Are you quiet and hard-working? Are you usually messy, or do you care a lot about being polished and proper at all times? Would you rather spend the day cracking jokes or being serious and thinking deeply? There's no right answer to any one of these questions because everybody is different, but asking them can give you some clues about yourself. Rather than trying to fit in some mold or stereotype you think you need, drill down on what makes you unique.

Suzy Batiz (CEO of Poo-Pourri) and I with other event attendees

The great part of knowing who you are is you don't have to hide or compensate for your so-called "weaknesses." You can accept them and focus on your strengths—and as you accept yourself, other people will accept you too.

When I think of myself and my own persona, I'd say that I'm honest, creative and a straight-shooter—people might even think I'm a little bit rude sometimes because of how direct I am, but I always tell the truth. I tell people what they need to know, no matter what their reaction is going to be. Because of those qualities and because I know I have them, I can navigate many different personal and professional landscapes and can switch between them with ease. There's no magic to it: it's owning you are instead of pretending to be someone else.

Usually when people are networking, their body is there while mentally they've left the building. They have to put on a face or force themselves to smile to match the energy of the room, or they have to stiffen their posture and cross their arms to look equally serious as the people around them. It's the wrong way to go about things entirely. Speaking personally, I've sat at tables with the CEO of Target and the founder of Model Sports before and had dinner with them in sweatpants and a T-shirt while they were in suits. The point of saying that isn't to brag but to make a point; it's not how you look or how you act; it's about how authentic you are, your attitude and what you bring to the table.

Even though you can get away with dressing casually and being your authentic self if you have enough confidence, you need a good understanding of your environment to pull it off— and you also don't want to overcorrect the other way. You don't want to show up to your first interview in a tuxedo (trust me, I've seen that happen).

Key & Important Takeaways:

- Networking is only difficult if you have problems with your self-image.
- Everyone experiences imposter syndrome; the best way to avoid it is to be authentic.
- Accepting yourself helps you accentuate your strengths, which builds confidence.
- With enough confidence, what you say becomes less important.

Learning to Speak the Language

Obviously, there are some limits to acting however you want in a business or professional environment. You may be able to wear what you want if you're great at what you do, but you won't get very far if people don't take you seriously. One thing that many people learn the hard way as they get more successful is that being in the right rooms comes with a kind of language you have to understand. In other words, you need to be fluent in business jargon and formal business chatter even if you choose not to speak it very much.

The conversations you have with people in the corporate world are often stiff and unnatural, and you don't need to completely imitate it to move in that world, but you do need to know what stereotypical "adult talk" sounds like. Even if it comes with a level of formality you don't resonate with, it's powerful to be able to understand what the others are saying, roll with it and then pivot to control the conversation your own way. It doesn't mean you can't walk up to a millionaire, crack a joke about their outfit and laugh if that's who you are. If you have the confidence and can "speak the language," whatever you say and do will translate.

The most important thing to know about business-speak is that the person you're talking with might not use it, and you don't have to use it—but at least some of the people around you probably will. It's a necessary skill in networking and in business, and it extends to knowing how to open and close text messages and how to write emails appropriately as well. In Western business, it's all about how quickly and efficiently you can get things done without wasting time.

For example, if you're writing a business email, just stay professional and get right to the point:

Hello [Name]

I hope you're well. I'd like to discuss your thoughts on the slide deck I sent over earlier this week. Are you available Friday for a meeting at 2 pm?

You start with a formal introduction and name the person you're speaking to, and then give it a few spaces. After that, give a kind greeting and get into the meat of the email (the "ask" of it) right away. The more confident and direct you are, the better, but remember to be polite and don't be afraid to insert your own voice and charisma as you get to know people better. The point is there may come a day where your entire future depends on a single email or a single text message to a potential lead, and you want to know the basics for when that day comes. There's no need to be a perfectionist here—just know the rules and don't waste people's time.

Understanding the guidelines and foundations of communication in the business world before you jump in headfirst is crucial. I've seen so many people who could've landed millions and even billions of dollars in opportunities but who burned bridges because they couldn't be professional with the right people. Even if you're not particularly sensitive to these rules, the business world is.

Without going into too much detail, it's not hard to learn how to speak this way—all you have to do is look around and practice a little. Pay attention to how news anchors talk. Watch movies that have boardroom scenes. If you own stock in any big tech companies, listen in on one or two of their shareholder meeting calls (and if you don't own stock, buy a couple shares or search for old shareholder meetings online). Google keynote speeches from famous business people like Steve Jobs and Bill Gates. Even if it seems frustrating or unnecessary, the point of speaking and communicating a certain way ensures that everyone is at a certain standard, no matter what their background or culture. It's a level of formality that makes everything more effective when people come from all over the world.

As younger millennials and Gen Zers enter the marketplace, these formal standards are getting more and more relaxed over time; that follows for business clothing and style mores also. Regardless, there will always be those few very powerful people who are old-fashioned and who hold all the strings, so you must understand both worlds to be comfortable in either one. On the journey to success, you have to work with many people in many environments, and there's no need to be afraid of it (or of "the adult world"). The faster you understand how communication works, the faster you'll be able to network —and the faster you'll reach your goals.

Key & Important Takeaways:

- Even if your communication style is casual, learning to speak business is important.
- Mastering professional communication lets you walk in many different business worlds.
- Without mastering business communication, your success in business may become limited.

Use Youth To Your Advantage

When I was 14 years old, I remember landing my first client ever for my marketing and consulting business—the first who paid me for something other than photography. It was a Montessori school up the hill from my house that had hired me to do their social media, and I had to ride my bike over there every day to take photos for the posts. I knew I could provide value with the skills I had and make something of it. Online marketing to businesses was just another language I had to learn—and my creativity always tirelessly guided me through any challenge I took on.

As soon as I started, I wanted to launch a fully developed business right away, even though I didn't have the right infrastructure or understanding. I didn't know how to present myself. I didn't know how to get on a call. I didn't know the etiquette behind communicating with people, and I couldn't pretend like I did. I didn't even know what an invoice was at that time! Ultimately, I was getting ahead of myself. Rather than trying to do everything at once, I needed to be in the moment and set my ego and big visions aside. I had to learn the little things first so I could do everything in the right order.

After a while, I had to listen and be open to tough communication. People were blunt and honest with me, and I learned and improved. I started leveraging my age to get myself in rooms. I noticed that as a young person, people weren't looking at me like I was a threat—and that was where I saw my first really huge opportunity. After my first few clients, I got the chance to help a company give marketing services to other brands. It was a way of helping an established business understand social media from a younger perspective.

Right away, I saw that they ran their business casually around me because I was so young, and they didn't think I was paying attention. In meetings and calls, they were going over detailed ins and outs of their operation—specific figures, details about other team members and so much more. It was all confidential information, and I was too young to sign a non-disclosure agreement. They knew they were taking a risk by having me in the room but ultimately, they were writing me off.

What I learned from that experience was not to hoard information to use against them, just that I had more of an advantage in a so-called "adult" environment than I thought I did (and to this day, I still hold my phone on business calls like one of the owners of that company did).

Even if that experience was a little uncomfortable or unnerving at the time, it helped me get ahead. It helped me see the landscape of the business world I was entering in a low-pressure, protected way. I saw how people took phone calls, held meetings, greeted people in a business context, managed a business calendar and so on. In conversations, many of them let the conversation flow easily both ways, whereas many younger people I saw tried to control the conversation, which came off as weak or untrustworthy. I was absorbing it all.

After that experience, I practiced what I learned by doing cold calls, practicing sales techniques and measuring my success against some of the clients I worked for. Because of the phone skills I'd observed, I was handling calls better and closing more business. The original experience might've been uncomfortable, but it all helped me grow.

Key & Important Takeaways:

- Being young in an older business world has advantages and disadvantages.
- A disadvantage is that you may have more to learn and will need to face direct criticism and feedback.
- The advantage is people will often underestimate you, and what you learn will put you years ahead of others.

Getting Started by Getting Started

In the beginning of breaking into the business world, I was very concerned about my appearance and my age in some of the rooms I was in. As I got more experienced, I realized the truth: nobody cares about what you look like or how authentic you're coming off because everyone else in the room is concerned about how *they're* coming off. Everyone is doing the same thing. The key to success in networking, as in any other part of life or business, isn't some special technique. It's the ability to let go of your fear.

Whenever someone starts something new, the instinct is to try to be perfect—or at least to avoid ever being wrong. That mindset leads to overcomplicating situations and getting paralyzed to the point where you never actually get anything done. Instead, give yourself permission to go for it and let go of the fear of messing up. It's all a part of learning, and the process should be fun!

Don't punish yourself over your tiny mistakes like walking in front of a meeting the wrong way or writing a clumsy email. There's a balance to obtain in learning how to anticipate and navigate your environment and in letting the small things go. Ultimately, the faster you can understand the big concepts and systems—there are very few of them, so it's not that complicated—the sooner you can walk in the world in a way that fits your personality.

Though I've said it before and will say it again, every job

placement, opportunity or career move I've made was partly a result of networking to build in "back door" opportunities. Even after meeting Mark Cuban, I ended up working for his companies directly and was probably the youngest person in the building!

None of that would've been possible if I had actually "applied" for a job through the front door; it all depended on personal conversations, the reputation I'd built for myself and my relationships with other people. What's crucial is that you find your own back doors to reach your own goals. In all, the final goal is to work the right angles so you can show up anywhere as yourself. It is the most important thing.

Key & Important Takeaways:

- If you care too much about how you appear to others, remember everyone else is worried about the same thing.
- Don't try to be perfect when starting a new project— embrace small mistakes as learning opportunities.
- There's no secret about how to get started; you just have to get started.

CHAPTER 12

LEARN TO SELL

In seventh grade, I was part of a school program called Hoops for Heart. It was a national fundraiser that involved kids shooting hoops for charity. For every basket the kids made, sponsors would pledge some amount of money. There were prizes for whoever could raise the most money, and they were things like iPads and Kindles. I really wanted to win an iPad, so I decided I would go as hard as I could for the top prize.

I spent my free time researching where all the rich neighborhoods were, what doors I should knock on and how to get through gated communities. I started by knocking on doors in my neighborhood because I already had relationships with people—what's called a "warm audience" in sales terms. I went door to door, letting them know who I was and that I was raising money for the American Heart Association through Hoops for Heart.

In a few weeks, I had knocked on 150 to 200 doors. In the beginning, I leveraged the fact that I lived in the neighborhood to get my foot in the door for donations of some sort. If they started hesitating or pulling away, I would say something like, "Even if it's a dollar, that's fine—it will go a long way." I had many different scripts in my mind that I used depending on the situation, all put together based on trial, error and intuition.

As I got further from my house, I started leveraging the fact that other people in the neighborhood were also donating to me. I had a piece of paper that had the names of donors on it and the amount they pledged to keep track of all the accounting. (Looking back, I didn't realize how dangerous it was for an unaccompanied seventh-grader to wander all over the city knocking on random people's doors, but that's beside the point.)

I kept documenting donations, and naturally I started to realize if one of my neighbors saw a big donation above the line they were writing on, they were more likely to donate more. For example, if Tommy donated $10, Bob would be more likely to donate $20. But there was a cap to that effect in that it wouldn't go past $100 (except for a few occasions).

As I took advantage of the fact that people were outbidding each other, I also started trying to use some of the no's I was getting in a creative way as well. When people told me they wouldn't donate, I would ask, "What's your first name? I just want to make sure I don't come back to your house." After that, I would write their name down and write some random number down I could show the next person I asked (though I would later scribble out the fake number).

To try and get more than one person at a time, I would walk up to lines of people with the American Heart Association pamphlets in my hands and ask the first person for a donation. If that person said no, I knew the five people behind them would most likely say no also. If someone said yes, there was a much higher chance that someone behind that first person would say yes also—the chances of success would increase by 50 or 60 percent.

I didn't realize it at the time, but all the strategies I was using in seventh grade were teaching me the fundamentals of sales. I ended up winning first place in the state! At the end of it all, I won the iPad along with all the other prizes, and it hadn't even been close—I had outplaced the person in second place by almost $3000.

All other skills aside, sales are the backbone of any business you can imagine. Without sales, there's no money coming in; if there's no money, there's no revenue, and there's no ability to grow. Really, there's no ability to do much of anything except make a sale however you can.

I've heard a lot of people say, "I hate sales," which never made sense to me. We are always selling something. When you get pulled over, you're selling the officer on not giving you a speeding ticket. When you're negotiating a raise, you're selling your value to the company you work for. When you're writing a college application essay, you're selling yourself to the institution.

Ultimately, sales turn the world—and when I realized that, it didn't take long for me to get into marketing so I could get better at it. Having that viewpoint, it confuses me when people take such a negative approach—why would anyone hate or be afraid of the very thing that makes money move?

Like networking, "sales" can be a dirty word if people misunderstand it. Sometimes, being a salesperson or "working in sales" has the connotation of tricking people into buying things they don't want or pulling the wool over someone's eyes. That's not what good salespeople do—at all. Good salespeople are good at persuading others, but they start with making an authentic connection with them and understanding their needs. In reality, sales are behind almost everything we do at every step of life, even for people who don't run a business.

Key & Important Takeaways:

- People look down on sales, but we are always selling ourselves in different parts of life.
- Without good sales, no money can come in, and businesses can't function.
- Good sales aren't about tricking people; it's about authentic connection and communication.

Visualizing Your Back Door To Successful Sales

As with goal-setting, one of the biggest keys to good sales is visualization. Whenever someone buys something or is talked into doing something, they have to have a vision of what their life will be like after. Similarly, the person selling something has to present a very clear story and vision of what that life is, a vision that the other person believes and wants to jump into. The common misconception about sales is that it has to be a very direct, confrontational part of business. Instead, you can use visualization to create a "back door" in your sales process—and you can use it on others and yourself.

When you have a visual in your head of something you want to achieve, it takes a lot of selling to actually make it a reality for yourself. You have to talk to people who are gatekeepers of that opportunity and get them to let you in—whether those gatekeepers are people, companies, situations or anything else.

Whatever the case, it's a kind of door that you need to walk through to get where you're going, and once it opens, everything starts to fall into place. Getting the door open is the hardest part (and more often than not, it's networking that opens the door). It's the part where you actually get an important figure to sit down with you, or you pull the right strings to set up an introduction. Sales can only come after that part of the work is done.

To get to that point, you need to sell the vision of what you want done to yourself first. After you've imagined what all the sales and networking and marketing can do for you and your life, you will have the emotional energy you need to sell it to others—it's the same concept as using visualization in your goal-setting. The more time you spend building out your visualizations, the better you will be at selling things once you understand the basics of sales skills.

Key & Important Takeaways:

- Like goal-setting, visualization is important to sales as well.
- Strong visualization helps you anticipate gatekeepers and get past them.
- Before you sell the product or service, you sell the vision.

Ethos, Logos, Pathos

There's no one way of selling people things—even if some sales gurus might disagree. I approach sales with a few simple principles you may recognize from any high school English class—there are only a few important concepts and systems to master, and you can put them to use everywhere. The ancient Greek concept of rhetoric everyone learns still holds up thousands of years later as a great foundation for sales. To close any sale, you have to use at least one of these pieces (if not all three).

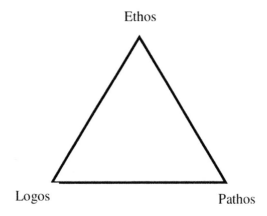

Ethos

Logos   Pathos

It's a system that works well for me, but I'm always adding to my arsenal. In any case, here's a refresher:

Ethos: At the top of the triangle is ethos, and it refers to the "spirit" of your message. It's the credibility, trust and personal connection that the speaker or seller has with the listener or customer. Anyone who doesn't try to form a strong connection with their customers risks losing their trust—and anyone who doesn't trust you definitely won't buy something from you. In a more practical sense, this is the part of sales that includes personal branding, confidence, speaking skills and other people's words—meaning testimonials, introductions made by other people and an approving network that connects the dots.

Logos: Logos represents logic and structure in an argument or sale. Once you've established that familiarity, you need to build a case about how whatever you're selling works and how it will actually help the other person. It's a very important part of the triangle, but it's the part that amateur salespeople focus on the most and at their own peril. It's good to use case studies, numbers, percentages and facts to convince a person's logical mind what they should do, but you don't want to "logic" the people you're selling to death. A better way to think of it is in terms of using metaphors and analogies rather than just cold facts to close a deal. You can still appeal to someone in a very pragmatic way that shows them how something works without boring them or getting too technical.

Pathos: Finally, pathos is the emotional aspect of the sale—and it can also be one of the more elusive elements. While it's easy to show someone why what you're selling is helpful or that other people think it's helpful, the real challenge is to show the emotional impact it will have on their life. In some ways, pathos brings the other two elements together. What story are you telling? What vivid language are you using? What kind of verbal judo can you throw at the sale to wrestle everything into one package? If you can master all three of these elements, you will have the fundamentals you need to pursue new sales with confidence.

When you put all three of these together, you can use them to analyze your sales scripts to see how well you're doing. If you had to sell a water bottle and wanted to use all three pieces, it might go something like this:

"You seem thirsty—and if you're not, you will be soon. I have this water bottle that I think you're going to want. Yes, this water bottle may look a little beat up, but I saved just enough for you. This water is the go-to brand for some of the most powerful people in the world (adding a layer of mystique here). I was skeptical about it too at first and almost walked away as someone was telling me this very story, but I stuck around, and what I heard changed my life. It turns out that this water comes from the cleanest source in the world! It has been tested by scientists of all kinds, which is what makes it so expensive—but it's totally worth it. If I were you, I'd be

grabbing this out of my hands right now—but it's not yours just yet."

This is just one simple example, but if you read it closely, you can see some of the techniques of ethos, logos and pathos at work. The reason I won't break this paragraph down too much further is because it isn't meant to be memorized. Instead, use the three elements mentioned and see if you can see where each one is working in the paragraph.

What do you think is working well about it, and what's intriguing? If you were selling the water bottle, what parts of this script would you use, and what would you change? If you can start applying these skills in your daily life and practicing with examples like the above, you'll hone your own sales skills in no time.

Key & Important Takeaways:

- Selling anything requires logic, emotion and credibility.
- In any sales pitch, all three aspects have to be represented in the language of the pitch.
- There is no one perfect sales pitch since all clients and products are different—experimentation is key.

CHAPTER 13

PRACTICE GOOD LEADERSHIP

"Know yourself and you will win all battles." -Sun Tzu

A lot of this book is about what you can do to take control over your own life—but at a certain level of success, you will hit a plateau without great people by your side. To accomplish huge things, you need an entire team of people who believe in the same vision and who can execute it. You have to make sure everyone feels safe to take risks, be honest and give their best efforts. In short, to have a great team, you need to have amazing leadership skills.

As you get further in life, your ability to run a team is so important. Ultimately, every company is really just a team or a set of teams. They work inside the company and outside it, making sure everything runs smoothly. If you are going to be the person with the vision who builds those teams, you have to make sure you can get people to listen to you and believe in you. You have to create a good workplace culture where they can use their skills to the fullest and feel like they're valuable. At the same time, you can't create a workplace that is completely like the Wild West where everyone does whatever they want with no structure. There's a balance to strike, and it takes time to learn.

From a very early age, I always wanted to be a leader. I took responsibility for things in school. I joined a lot of extracurricular activities, and I headed up projects whenever I could. As I got older, I pursued leadership training opportunities through the Boy Scouts and workshops to hone those skills because I knew they would be valuable. I always had a vision for my life, and I knew what it would take to achieve it. Those are the same core traits you need to be a good leader.

Leaders need to be visionaries and good communicators—and anyone who can't be those two things probably shouldn't lead a team. Still, the best leaders also lead by example and can follow just as much as they lead. If you're the CEO and you're telling your whole team not to use cell phones during meetings, but you're always on yours, your team members will follow your behavior. Why would they listen to you if you're not following your own rules? How all these elements work together depends on your personality and the personalities of the people around you. It comes down to values and leadership styles.

Key & Important Takeaways:

- Taking control of your life is good, but without people helping you, you will plateau.
- At higher levels of success, leading teams becomes a very important skill.
- To be an effective leader, you must practice what you preach.

The Pros and Cons of Seven Common Leadership Styles

For any given problem, there are plenty of ways to approach

solving it. Some situations require more flexibility while others need more control; others need kindness while some require swift action. Mixing and matching these different techniques and strategies makes for a truly great leader—but first, it helps to understand the basics of all of them.

1. Authoritarian or Autocratic Leadership

Of all the styles, this is the most aggressive and most control-oriented. You can think of it like a country that has a dictator who is above laws and rules that would slow them down, where as soon as one person says something, everyone else moves in that direction. It might not be great to be in a country led by someone like that, but it's a style with pros and cons all the same.

Pros: Because this style is so strict and decisive, it means that big, complex decisions can be made very quickly. There's no debating or waffling; instead, it's all action. Though you don't need to do this all the time, being more authoritarian can be useful in a time crunch or when efficiency is priority number one.

Cons: Obviously, it's easy to see the drawbacks of this style. Being too authoritarian will make people afraid of you, which can breed resentment or distrust, hurt team performance and maybe even make people conspire against you. It's also a very rigid style of dealing with teams. It doesn't open the door for open communication, collaboration, new ideas or much creativity.

2. Democratic Leadership

Democratic leadership is a much more team-oriented way

of leading and making decisions where communication is open, and everyone participates in the process. When a big choice needs to be made, the main leader may meet with ten or so other key team members who all propose ideas that are put to a vote.

Pros: Unlike authoritarian leadership, this style lets everyone feel like they're part of the process and is much more open to collaboration and communication. It also allows teams the ability to be more creative and innovative since so many things are discussed and picked apart before big decisions are made.

Cons: Since this is the opposite of authoritarian leadership, the drawbacks are also the opposite. When you consider every opinion and every feeling someone on your team has, your efficiency and speed drop a lot. If things are too democratic, you run the risk of seeming weak when making big decisions or of not getting anything done.

3. Laissez-Faire Leadership

This "hands-off" style takes democratic leadership even further by having teams with as little centralized control as possible. Instead of putting big decisions to a vote or making them all at once, the team might meet to discuss a priority and then send everyone off in their own direction to work on it using their skills.

Pros: The biggest upside of this style is that you let your team members use their skills and strengths to the fullest, with the potential of getting the best possible work out of them. It opens the door to creativity in a huge way, particularly if you have many strong creatives working for you with their own visions. It can also create a very strong workplace culture of trust, which encourages innovation.

Cons: The cons here are obvious: the potential for disaster is high for inexperienced team members or inexperienced leaders. Letting everyone do what they want is great if everyone is skilled, focused and committed to the same vision; if they're not, it means nothing gets done, the company goes in all directions, and chaos rules the day.

4. Strategic Leadership

Unlike some of the other styles, strategic leadership is more analytical and technical. The biggest decisions the company makes may be more objective and less based on instinct. It requires the main leader to have an in-depth understanding of each different part of the company and to make careful, timed decisions that will benefit every aspect of it in the long term.

Pros: This approach is good for using real information to build confidence and to track progress towards goals. It can also be helpful for very complex goals or projects when many different teams need to come together and synthesize lots of different information.

Cons: The main drawback of this style is that it runs the risk of being uninspired and less innovative. While it may help to use lots of data or strategy to make big decisions, sometimes there is no data available for the most defining decisions we have to make about the future.

5. Visionary Leadership

This style can be a blend of some of the other styles, but it mostly means that the person in charge has a very big-picture vision of the company's potential, one that may be totally different than what the company is today. These leaders set huge goals and imagine things that haven't been done yet, all while guiding their teams to realize their vision.

Pros: In the best cases, the pros are that these companies are the most interesting and fulfilling to work for. Good visionary leaders inspire the people around them, make them feel important and help push them beyond what they thought possible—with a very high potential for creativity and innovation.

Cons: In bad cases, visionary leadership can go off the rails. The leader can lose touch with reality or fall out of communication with their team, sending everyone off in their own directions and hurting team morale. It is also a kind of "all or nothing" commitment—and if the team stops believing, they may leave or give up on a project.

6. Coaching Leadership

This style is also a blend and falls somewhere between democratic and laissez-faire. In coaching, team members aren't micromanaged on their day-to-day tasks, but they are guided towards discovering their own strengths and hitting medium and long-term goals. It also comes with leaders who understand the psychology of their team members deeply and who use that to get the best results.

Pros: The benefits of a good coach can't be understated, so the same is true with this leadership style. When done right, all key team members can be fully engaged and put to work on tasks they will be best at. They will feel invested in, and their skills will always be developing and improving.

Cons: One big drawback with this style is that not all coaches are equally good. As a result, this method may take a long time to pay off—or it might not work at all in some cases. Similarly, developing your team members' skills on a deep individual level also means that you give them more power to walk away from you if you don't have a structure in place to keep your best people.

7. Servant Leadership

This style has become more popular recently and is a very people-focused approach to business. While this can still be a strong leadership style, the focus is that the most powerful leader in the company will try to make themselves the least powerful in some crucial ways—by making sure they put the team members ahead of themselves and by making sure everyone is as personally and professionally satisfied as they can be.

Pros: The biggest pro of this approach is that it is very empowering to team members and that it creates very strong loyalty. When team members feel like they can be their full selves and use their full talents, they work better with one another and produce better work in the long term as well.

Cons: Unlike some of the others, the main drawback of this style is the difficulty that comes with it. Many strong leaders have big egos (as do many high-performing team members). For inexperienced leaders, managing all those egos together smoothly can be very challenging and overwhelming. If the leaders can't balance strength and compassion, they run the risk of being taken advantage of.

The truth is nobody is just one of these styles all the time, and all of them have their own uses. The key is to see which one of these most fits your personality and your values and to move between them depending on the situation.

Key & Important Takeaways:

- Leaders can choose between many different styles of leadership to achieve their goals.
- Different situations call for different styles— sometimes with more control and sometimes with less.
- The best leaders understand the basics of all styles and can move between them as necessary.

Building the Perfect Team

Just like there are leadership styles, there are also different kinds of team members—and it can be difficult to make different team members mesh if you don't have a system in place. While some people are very creative and lack discipline and organization, others are all about details but get lost when it comes to big-picture thinking. When you're just starting out, it's common to have a team of people you already know or people you've done business with, but they might not work well together. To get around this, you need a system to sort people, so you know their skills will complement each other.

While every company and leader can have their own way of doing this, one of the best and most straightforward comes from Kathy Kolbe. Kolbe is the founder of Kolbe Corp, but she's most known in the business world for a test she developed to assess team members. The test is called the Kolbe A Index, which asks potential team members 36 questions to get a read on their instincts behind decision-making. Some people are more focused on details and getting information; others are focused on putting their head down and powering through any obstacle. None of these ways is right or wrong, but everyone has their own unique combination—and every team needs a balance of all of them.

Regardless of what method you use to put your team together, you need to find people who complement each other and who can develop their own styles of team leadership within the company, so you don't have to control everything yourself. Today, I could walk away from my company for an extended period, and it would keep running. The people second in charge have a lot of power, and I encourage them to use their skills to make decisions. A lot of people are scared to do this, but I find that people should be empowered to do that —and it makes my life easier as well.

I don't want a team of followers. I want people who are both leaders and followers because that is a perfect hybrid. You want people who are motivated to work with clients and their success, not just people who are there to collect a paycheck. That's what excites me so much about running a company: building a team that can accomplish huge things together! To do that, you have to build an innovative culture where people are motivated by goals and not by surface benefits—but it can be very hard to find those people.

I've toured major companies and seen so many examples of how *not* to run things. In one case, I was touring a company with a young intern named Kevin, who worked on the 16th floor of the building. Though he was showing me around, he was also complaining a lot about all the problems with management and how they ran things. The company had an open floor plan that was so extreme they didn't even let employees have desks—only people who worked in the C-suite had their own locked offices. All the lower-level employees had to clear their desks out every day. They were basically working in a WeWork until they made it to the very top levels of the company!

It was clear that Kevin and the other employees were so frustrated and annoyed by the process—and he said it was showing in the company's decision-making. I had come to the company to give some marketing insights for a younger demographic, but Kevin was already warning me to keep my expectations low. He told me that lots of people at the company who weren't executives had ideas about how to change or improve things, but they were all scared to bring their ideas up to the people who could execute them. There were even bosses at the company who wouldn't take ideas up the food chain because they were scared of losing their job.

The reason that culture had developed made sense if you looked at the money. Lots of employees there were paid through stock incentives that only unlocked after they worked for a longer period of time, which prevented them from taking any risks. If you were about to unlock a bunch of stock worth hundreds of thousands of dollars and sail off into retirement, why would you risk all of that by listening to some stupid intern's idea that could get you fired? All of it was a clear lesson to me: if you don't get your culture right, you will fail.

If someone is afraid to speak up at your company, you've failed at building a good culture. If people can't come in on the first day and talk to the CEO, the chain of command is broken. So many people and companies rely on ego and credibility to get things done, but all of that is backward. Respect is important, but great ideas should be able to make it all the way to the top of the company and be heard at a moment's notice. Many companies can't do that, but some companies can—and those are the ones that win.

Key & Important Takeaways:

- Like leadership styles, team members have different styles of working and understanding as well.
- Kolbe tests are a good way to screen new team members and build teams.
- Different types of teams and leaders produce different work cultures.
- Achieving the right balance is crucial because bad work culture can break a company.

The Cycles of Team Building

Balancing leadership and team-building isn't easy, but it's helpful to know that there are patterns that everybody will experience. Whenever you bring a new team together, you are bound to run into conflict—but that's not a sign that you've made a mistake or that something is wrong. Many people are afraid of conflict in their teams, but conflict can be good! The easiest way to understand is to think of team-building in cycles, because it's how all teams come together to perform their best.

This process happens in four stages:

Forming: In this stage, the team is brand-new and still getting to know each other. Because there aren't strong bonds between anyone yet—and there aren't bonds between the team as a whole—everything will be confusing, and everyone may seem a bit disconnected from each other. It's natural that some small groups might start to form after a while. They have their own goals and ways of doing things not in line with the whole team's vision or interest. In those cases, it takes a good leader to encourage the team to bond more with one another and gather around one plan of action or one direction.

Storming: After the initial disconnected stage, there may be one core leader in the group that everyone is looking to for guidance. By this stage, everyone has identified some of their own strengths and has sorted themselves in the group hierarchy. Now there will be more group discussions about goals and priorities—and also a lot more conflict as different ideas come to a head. Still, this "storming" is a natural part of teams discovering how everyone thinks and what people's strengths are. Ideally, the leader won't try to control this too much and will let the team work things out among each other.

Norming: After that first bumpy period of communication challenges and conflict, the team will start to develop a stronger sense of shared culture, and the core leader might not be as necessary anymore. Instead of always asking one person for solutions to every problem, team members might start to ask one another and discuss ideas on their own. In this stage, there is more productive back-and-forth between team members and more community—and the best thing the leader can do is to allow this process to happen and not try to seize the control back.

Performing: Finally, the "performing" stage is where the team finally finds its best structure and leadership. Everyone understands everyone else on the team, and there is natural leadership among each team. Rather than just having one team, the team works more like several interconnected teams at once, all pushing each other forward.

SWOOP Teams Maturity Model

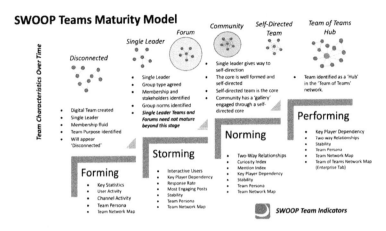

With these four stages in mind, you can look at the people around you and see how far along you are in developing as a team. All of these stages are natural, but not all teams successfully make it through to the end. Part of it takes a good combination of people, and part of it takes a leader who knows when to step in and when to back away. The final thing to remember is that any time you add a new team member to this equation, the entire process starts all over again—which is why it pays to keep your team members happy and working well together!

Key & Important Takeaways:

- When new teams are formed, there is always conflict —but that isn't necessarily a bad thing.
- A team's abilities develop in predictable stages, getting more connected and in sync as they grow.
- Adding or removing team members can throw off the entire balance and make you start over—so keeping your teams happy is crucial.

Avoiding the NASA O-Ring

In 1986, NASA launched the Challenger space shuttle, and everyone gathered by their TVs to watch. There was a spectacular buildup to the event, and everyone was excited to see what America's best and brightest minds had accomplished together. Unfortunately, the shuttle exploded in the air just 76 seconds after takeoff, killing the seven crew members onboard and shocking everybody who was watching. The worst part of the disaster not everybody remembers is it all could have been avoided.

The reason the shuttle exploded had to do with its O-ring, a circular gasket that was used to seal one of the rocket boosters. Because it was too cold during the launch, the O-ring had been damaged during liftoff and led to the boosters exploding. It was a potential problem that NASA's engineers had pointed out months before the launch, but when they brought it up to their managers, they were ignored. According to what the project managers thought, the statistical odds of the part failing or the shuttle exploding were astronomically low, so there was no issue in going ahead. Part of the problem was internal leadership and communication, and the other was how they had assessed risk. In all of it, there is a serious lesson about how leadership and internal communication can go wrong.

Because of a culture of groupthink developed in some parts of NASA at that time, people died as a result. In my own life, I try to remember that when it comes to business. I may not be working on space projects, but the danger of not delivering for a client because of bad leadership or bad workplace culture is always there. It's why I've encouraged the people I work with to come to me with any idea or criticism so we can always improve.

I've had my own employees tell me very directly that a project didn't look good, and I always appreciate it. If I know what's going on, I have the chance to fix problems that come up, and I can always be improving. As I've learned, people need to be able to voice their thoughts without censorship. When you only lead through demands and control, it sets you up for failure. You have to be humble enough to listen to feedback because lots of good things get left behind when you're close-minded.

Just because you're good doesn't mean you're the best, and there are always smarter ways of doing just about anything. To really lead a team, you need to make sure everyone feels involved and has ownership. You want people to work hard because they want to and because they believe in the project, not because they're afraid of failure.

Key & Important Takeaways:

- Groupthink can shut down open communication within a company and ruin product launches.
- Even the highest-achieving teams can become susceptible to groupthink and communication breakdowns.
- To avoid these problems, leaders need to be humble enough to accept honest feedback.

CHAPTER 14

LIVE LIFE TO THE FULLEST

Whether your life plan is to build a massive company that reinvents the way we do things or to use your skills to break free of a 9-to-5, it's important to stay focused on what really matters. There's an old saying that fits in both life and business, and once you've mastered everything else, it helps to think of it again and again:

"The main thing is to keep the main thing the main thing."

There are plenty of great ideas out there and plenty of reasons to start a business to bring one of them to life—but at the core of it all is a deeper "why" that only you can know. It's the secret part of what drives you and what you love, and it comes from a place of deep self-motivation.

For me, self-motivation came from many places. I was told "no" a lot growing up, but I didn't trust the answers I was getting. I didn't think the people telling me "no" were accurate, and so I challenged authority constantly. I used to sneak into concert venues or other exclusive events just to show other people it could be done (though I had to stop doing that as I got older and people started to recognize me). Ultimately, I didn't want to be put on any of the career paths that were laid out for me, but I also didn't want that to mean I would live a small life. The result was that I turned into an outlier.

I was never following the same road as everyone else—I was on a gravel path next to the main road, going in my own direction. Being on that gravel road can be scary, lonely and isolating at times—but even so, gravel roads lead to the tops of mountains. There are plenty of people who start up the mountain but turn back as they get closer because the road ahead looks too difficult to climb.

At the top of the mountain, life is the best—you have great networks, you are surrounded by amazing people, and you're living out your dreams. Not many people are willing to take the journey, and to be honest, I'm still climbing that mountain. People say there's not a lot of space at the top, but there actually is because so few people are willing to make the trek. Once you're there, you can truly control your own life. All the hard work you put in finally pays off, and you can start putting energy back into the things that make you tick—things that don't even need a reason behind them.

One of the best things about all the work I've done in building a business and branding myself is that I can travel almost as much as I want to—so just to inspire you to live your own life to the fullest in your own way, I'm going to share some travel tips I've learned over the years.

Key & Important Takeaways:

- Starting a business is a great goal, but an even greater goal is to live a good life.
- Following your own path is crucial to starting your own business, but it can be a lonely experience; the same is true of life.
- Though walking off the beaten path can be lonely and difficult at times, it offers greater rewards than anything else.

Travel the World with Ease

Whether you're headed to college, work, fun or family, you'll likely find yourself flying there—which can be stressful and difficult if you're not prepared. Fortunately, I have seven rules I follow to make every journey a breeze:

1. Be prepared. When you get to the airport, you are going to be put in security lines and treated like cattle, so you might as well prepare for it. Wear shoes you can slip off easily. Have your ID out and your boarding pass in hand. Put your cell phone, watch and other metal items in your bag or ready to place in a bin. Have your laptop ready to pull out and place in a bin by itself. This is not a time where you can sit down and repack, so arrange your belongings accordingly before you arrive.

2. Arrive early. It's the worst feeling ever to miss a flight and not make it to your meeting or event. Getting to the airport 40 minutes before boarding will allow you enough time to chill out and get some food after making it through security.

3. If you can't lift it over your head, it is *not* a carry-on. When you board the plane, everyone is rushing to get seated and settled. No one has time for you to attempt to pick up your 100-pound bag and place it in the overhead bin. Plus, doing so is simply unsafe since when you land, you'll have to pull it behind you and could hit someone with it.

4. If you're likely to use the restroom, take the aisle seat.
Climbing over other passengers or asking them to stand up so you can get out is always awkward, and for that reason alone, the aisle seat is underrated. I always sit on the outside so I can get a full view of what's happening on the plane.

5. Be observant. If the people sitting next to you or around you have a book, earphones or they look busy, don't try to force a conversation. It can be difficult, but it's best to keep your thoughts to yourself, so you don't drive people around you crazy.

6. Be patient. I have had to board and get off the same plane three times because of bad weather before, which is a good lesson that things don't always go as planned. Complaining and yelling at customer service won't speed things up either. When you land, don't jump up and think you're in some kind of race. Everyone will get off eventually, so for the love of God, don't push.

7. Respect personal space. Keep your feet and knees off the seat in front of you and only recline your seat if you know the person behind you won't get crushed or annoyed. Sometimes, it's a good thing to ask for permission.

Following these seven rules will help you and those around you, but to get even more specific, here are a few more tips to save you time and keep you happy:

- **Bring an empty water bottle.** TSA will make you throw away any water you have because of security. But you can still take an empty Nalgene with you! After you get through security, find a water fountain to fill it up. This will keep you hydrated — and save you from purchasing an overpriced bottle of water.
- **Pack an extra set of clothes and some wipes.** I have had someone spill an entire bottle of Sprite on me during a flight. Luckily, I had an extra set of clothes and baby wipes packed.
- **Bring a personal bag.** This is separate from your carry-on and should fit under your seat. A personal bag is ideal for holding items you might need in-flight, such as your laptop, earbuds, gum or a book. Choose something with a lot of pockets because this will help you stay organized.
- **During the flight, don't try to get your giant carry-on out of the overhead bin above someone's head.** Pull whatever you will need for the flight out before takeoff—or see the above point and bring a personal bag that can fit under your seat!
- **Bring noise-canceling headphones.** I cannot fly without my Bose QuietComfort 25, which helps block out the loud engine and other noises.
- **Apply for TSA precheck.** Even though it costs extra, the time you'll save with a quick, convenient security check is worth it.
- **Once you use your ID and wallet/purse, immediately put it back into your bag and zip it away.** The worst thing while traveling is to lose your credentials and money. It's also a good idea to have $20 to $100 in cash somewhere on you in case of an emergency.
- **Bring a jacket.** It gets cold when you are up in the

air, so make sure you have a light jacket with you so you can stay warm and happy.

- **Bring a battery pack, charging block and wire and place it in your backpack.** This will ensure you have enough power to get that Uber or make that phone call when you land.

I don't want to tell you how to live your dream life, but as you'll find out, even the fun parts can be more fun if you prepare and know the back doors to make them easier. I hope that anyone who follows all these life and business principles will realize their own power to shape their destiny. You don't have to listen to the people telling you to live a certain way or that you have to work a job you hate for 40 years and retire without enjoying life. In the age of the internet, anything is possible if you have the drive—and I hope to see you at the top of the mountain.

Key & Important Takeaways:

- When traveling or exploring, you can apply systems and routines to make everything easier and more fun.
- As in business, there are "back doors" to the fun parts of life as well.
- Nobody has to follow the same plan for their "dream life"—but achieving your personal dream life is the ultimate goal underneath everything else.

CONCLUSION

My entire life, I've always made decisions quickly. Sometimes I've made them too quickly, but I'd prefer that to the opposite because hesitation kills. It's easy to waste a lot of time thinking of all the angles of a decision or thinking about what will happen next if you take a risk. The way I see it, you can skip all that if you realize one thing: you're only one good decision away from changing your life. And that's my motivation.

Treating people well and believing in yourself will get you in the right rooms and offer you the right opportunities. Doing that again and again will change your life, so you should do it as often as possible. When I was younger, I dedicated myself to understanding personal development, communication, business, marketing and branding, and I never complained about it. It meant that I missed out on some things my peers were doing, like socializing and partying, but the result was that I bought my first house when I was 20 years old—and today, I work with major brands around the world and have a company I own that has been written about in Forbes and Entrepreneur. I don't know many people who can say that.

As I see it, there are two main routes in life. The first is you can get a standard education, go to college and become an employee. You can work your way up the chain, get in a relationship, save enough money for a house maybe, have kids and start the cycle over. It's the "white picket fence" model we're all familiar with, and many people go down that route. It's not necessarily the wrong route, but when you see into the lives of people who spend an average year's salary like Monopoly money, it puts everything in perspective.

The other route is to build something of your own. Maybe you go to college, or maybe you don't, but either way, you start learning in the real world, and you put yourself out there. You build a structure around yourself and your skills, and you find a team to help you take things to the next level. You learn to do your own thing, be your own boss and follow your own ideas.

More and more, the younger generation is choosing that route and becoming entrepreneurs, launching brands, becoming influencers and so on. The white picket fence is slowly rotting away because people are realizing that going in debt for life just to maybe get a raise in a decade while others outperform you is not enough.

It's a very exciting time to be young and in charge of your own life. With new technologies like cryptocurrency and NFTs, it's clear that people are building things that have real value and that are changing the world of business overnight. I've seen people turn into millionaires in weeks, if not days off the strength of some of these new ideas, and it makes me excited. Instead of having to pledge your loyalty to a giant company for years on end, these new opportunities are giving power back to people.

If you have it in you to take the risks and embrace the pain that goes with it, you can find your own route in life. There's still power in route one, by the way—it just doesn't have a monopoly on that power anymore.

You will still run into people saying things like, "What are you doing here? You're not a consultant! You don't have a degree!" Even today, I hear things like that all the time. From an outdated perspective, all some people can see is what they learned in business classes taught by professors who have been out of the real world for decades. The iPhone didn't even exist when most of them got their degrees! Social media didn't exist! Why would I be taught by someone who isn't a practicing person in the real world? Because they own an expensive piece of paper? That makes no sense to me.

Today, plenty of MBAs are struggling to find jobs because the market is flooded with them. The world is realizing that business schools are just a factory to print culturally "normal" people. These days, the people who come out of MBA programs are lacking a lot of important characteristics that you need to change the world—things like risk-taking, creativity and original thinking. It's not true for everyone, and it may sound harsh, but looking at the big picture, the trend is leaning away from the old ways of doing things.

Ultimately, you are in charge of your own life, and you can take whatever route you want to take. All I want to tell anyone who reads this book is if you are stuck in a system telling you you're not worth it or that you won't make it in life, you have the option not to listen. You have the option to believe in yourself, find a new environment and make your own choices. If you focus on yourself and your own strengths, you will find your own back doors to the life of your dreams—and you'll leave the cookie-cutter thinkers and the naysayers in the dust. I hope that for everyone who reads this.

Just remember that for any building you want to enter, there's always a back door. But you have to be the one to find it.

ACKNOWLEDGMENTS

I'd like to start off my acknowledgments by thanking the very people who brought me to life. My parents. They struggled so I could succeed; I can't even imagine the journey and risk they took leaving their home country behind and immigrating to the United States with only $450 in their pocket. I have learned the meaning of sacrifice and GRIT from my parents, and I have no words in the world that I can write down to thank them for all of their support over the years. Thank you, **Mom & Dad**; without your care and love, I wouldn't be where I am today.

Anish Goel is my little brother who is always there for me. He was the first person who read through this book and is the smarter half of me. I have been blessed to have called you my brother, and I cannot wait to see how you succeed and change the world in the coming years. To the best brother I could have ever asked for. Thank you, Anish.

You have always been there, no matter what. From the day I met you, you have been my travel buddy, my support system, my proofreader, and most importantly, my best friend ever. You are everything to me, and I am thankful for all the memories you have shared and for the many to come. Thank you, **Caryn Marjorie.**

Without you, this book wouldn't have been possible. Thank you for the teachings, access, and opportunities you have given me. You have given me more than I can ever ask for, and I am beyond thankful for the relationship we have. I can not wait to see the impact this book will have on the world. Thank you, **Joe Polish & the Genius Network Team!**

I'm eternally grateful to **Diana S. Zimmerman**, who responded to thousands of my emails over the past 11 years of my life. She allowed me to see the potential within myself. She motivated me to keep going in both school and all my business ventures. I followed in her footsteps to become a marketer and now an author. Thank you, Diana.

I called many photographers back when I was in the eighth grade, and you were the only person who called back. You taught me the values of business, work ethic and most importantly, how to show up and do an incredible job no matter what. You enabled me to grow in all aspects of my life and gave me opportunities to learn from my mistakes while being close enough to catch me if I ever needed backup. I want to thank **Nick Mallouf** for building my foundation in business.

Mark Cuban and the MCC Team (Nick Fragnito & EJ Williams) You trusted me to work side by side with you at the Mark Cuban Companies. Giving me the confidence to grow from the inside out. I learned the values of marketing and branding and shadowed the work of the incredible teams that run your brands. Thank you for the life-changing opportunity to learn from you and everyone around you!

The person who showed me the ins and outs of PR and media. You also taught me the values of patience and confidence as well as being prepared in business. Having the opportunity to work side by side with you showed me a new world of ways to do things, and for that, I am grateful. Thank you for all the support and mentorship, **Cheri Garcia.**

Thank you for taking the time to sit down with me and invite me over to the office so many times. You allowed me to connect with so many people and gave me the opportunity to photograph you in action. That was an incredible experience, and I always think back to that day. You are a warm force of energy and always supportive. Thank you, **Robert Corky Ray.**

To my friend, roommate, and fellow up-and-coming entrepreneur. Thank you for all the amazing memories and moments, from going to China to being all around LA with you. You have taught me the value of being nice to everyone. You know how to make anyone smile and feel like the biggest person ever. Thank you, **Casey Adams.**

A lot of the teachings and wisdom that I have developed around personal dev and mental health tools comes from these two. I want to give a special shoutout to **Michael & Deb Bernoff** for allowing me to attend their events and getting to know the ins and outs of how to become a better me.

From the day I met you, You taught me how to take my dreams and stop at nothing from turning them into a reality. You are an incredible person and give me the ability to learn how the world works. I will never forget the experiences and times we shared together. Thank you, **Justin Wright.**

I have had many teachers over the years, but only a few have changed the entire course of my life. Starting with **Mrs. Elkins** for seeing the potential in that trouble-making kid and enabling me to show my creative side, to **Christy Fuller** for showing me how to read correctly and sitting down with me for hours to get through my first book. **Diane de Waal** for showing me the beauty behind writing and crafting words into a story and **Robert Gribble** for trusting me and enabling me to run the largest club to ever exist at my high school in 50 years. Shoutout to **Sean Bagley** for being on my side no matter what!

Shoutout to **Alex Eason** and the **Student Emergency Response Team at Coppell High School.**

Last but not least. I was always prepared for the countless experiences I learned far outside my comfort levels in Boy Scouts. Achieving the rank of Eagle forever taught me how to be a good leader and an even better communicator. I want to give a huge shoutout to **Troop 840 (Circle 10)** in Coppell, Texas, for giving me the life skills to always BE PREPARED.

ABOUT THE AUTHOR

Ishan Goel is one of the top Gen Z marketers and the founder of Goel Strategies, a marketing agency specializing in branding and marketing strategy. Goel and his team work with startups and Fortune 500 companies alike. He has appeared in publications such as Forbes, The Huffington Post, Business Insider, Entrepreneur and many more.

Printed in Great Britain
by Amazon

80070732R00120